ALPHA BOOKS

FOOD FOR THE WORLD

NICOLA BARBER

Evans

EVANS BROTHERS LIMITED

This book is based on **Facing the Future**
FOOD FOR THE WORLD by Su Swallow,
first published by Evans Brothers Limited
in 1990, but the original text has been
simplified.

Evans Brothers Limited
2A Portman Mansions
Chiltern Street
London W1M 1LE

First published 1994
Reprinted 1995

Typeset by Fleetlines Typesetters, Southend-on-Sea
Printed in Hong Kong

ISBN 0 237 51367 6

Acknowledgements

Maps and diagrams – Jillian Luff of Bitmap Graphics
Illustrations – Outline Illustration, Derby – Andrew Calvert,
Andrew Cook, Andrew Staples
Design – Neil Sayer
Editor – Su Swallow
Language advisor – Suzanne Tiburtius

For their help and for information given the author and
publishers wish to thank the following:

Agricultural and Food Research Council (Institute of Food
Research, Institute of Plant Science Research and AFRC
Institute of Engineering Research); Oxfam Overseas Relief and
Development Organization; The London Food Commission;
Population Concern; The Association of Agriculture; ICI Seeds
and ICI Agrochemicals; Protan, Norway; Institute of
Oceanographic Sciences; InCA; FARM Africa; Intermediate
Technology; UN Food and Agriculture Organization; Hamish
Wilson; Guy and Teresa Sturtivant; David Field, Royal Botanic
Gardens, Kew.

For permission to reproduce copyright material the author and
publishers gratefully acknowledge the following:

Page 19 – ENDA TIERS MONDE, Dakar; page 25 – from a
diagram on New Scientist, London (1989); page 29 – (top)
AFRC Institute of Engineering Research; page 33 – from an
illustration by Gary Cook from *The Sunday Times*, July 16th
1989, © Times Newspapers Ltd. 1989; page 34 – from an
illustration by David Hart from, *The Times*, February 28th
1989, © Times Newspapers Ltd, 1989.

Cover – (left) Hank Morgan, Science Photo Library – (right,
from top) Jeremy Hartley, Intermediate Technology; Nigel
Cattlin, Holt Studios Ltd; Mark Edwards, Still Pictures.
Title page – Woman winnowing for seeds, Somalia – Hamish
Wilson.
Page 6 – (top) Mark Edwards, Still Pictures – (bottom) – Jeremy
Hartley, Intermediate Technology; page 7 – (top) Mark
Edwards, Still Pictures – (bottom) Norman Myers, Bruce
Coleman Limited; page 8 – Geoff Sayer, Oxfam; page 9 – Mary
Cherry, Holt Studios Ltd; page 10 – (top) Gerald Cubitt, Bruce
Coleman Limited – (bottom) Hamish Wilson; page 11 – (top)
Mark Edwards, Still Pictures – (bottom) Intermediate
Technology; page 12 – Nigel Cattlin, Holt Studios Ltd; page 13
– (top) Chris Prior, Seaphot Limited: Planet Earth Pictures –
(bottom) Philippe Plailly, Science Photo Library; page 14 – (left)
ICI Seeds – (right) Norman Owen Tomalin, Bruce Coleman
Limited; page 15 – Stephen Pern, The Hutchison Library; page
16 – Hamish Wilson; page 17 – Hamish Wilson; page 18 – (top)
Ashish Chandola, Survival Anglia – (bottom) Lee Lyon,
Survival Anglia; page 19 – (top) Hamish Wilson – (middle)
Francisco Erize, Bruce Coleman Limited; page 20 – (top) Gilbert
van Ryckevorsel, Seaphot Limited: Planet Earth Pictures –
(bottom) Michel Roggo, Bruce Coleman Limited – (inset) Hans
Reinhard, Bruce Coleman Limited; page 21 – (left, top right,
bottom right) Inigo Everson, Bruce Coleman Limited; page 23 –
(top) Protan, Norway – (bottom) Robert Jureit, Planet Earth
Pictures; page 24 – Nigel Cattlin, Holt Studios Ltd; page 25 –
(top left, top right, middle) Nigel Cattlin, Holt Studios Ltd;
page 26 – B. Brown, Planet Earth Pictures; page 27 – B. Brown,
Planet Earth Pictures; page 28 – (top) Massey-Ferguson –
(bottom) AFRC Institute of Engineering Research; page 29 –
(inset and bottom) AFRC Institute of Engineering Research;
page 30 – (top, bottom) Carl Schmidt-Luchs, Science Photo
Library; page 31 – (top, bottom) Prof. David Hall, Science Photo
Library; page 32 – (left) US Dept. of Energy, Science Photo
Library – (right) Agricultural and Food Research Council; page
34 – (top) ICI Seeds; page 35 – (top) Martini, Bruce Coleman
Limited – (bottom) Nigel Cattlin, Holt Studios Ltd; page 36 –
ICI Seeds; page 37 – Peter Casson, Planet Earth Pictures; page
38 – Terrence Moore, Susan Griggs Picture Agency; page 39 –
Hank Morgan, Science Photo Library; page 40 – Peter Menzel,
Wheeler Pictures, Colorific; page 41 – (top left, bottom left,
right) Peter Menzel, Wheeler Pictures, Colorific; page 42 – (left)
NASA, T.R.H. Pictures – (top right) NASA, T.R.H. Pictures –
(bottom right) The Telegraph Colour Library.

Contents

Introduction

We often see pictures of starving people in the newspapers and on television. These people usually live in countries where there is a **famine**. The people do not have enough to eat and many of them may die. Famines often happen in countries where there is not enough water to make the crops grow. When a famine happens, other countries may send money and food to help the starving people.

But it is not only in countries hit by famine that people are hungry. It is easy to forget that every day 750 million people do not have enough to eat. These people live mainly in the countries of Africa, Asia and Central and South America. These countries are often called the developing countries of the world. Developing countries are poor countries without much industry. People in the developing countries often have to grow all their own food. Sometimes the soil is poor and crops do not grow well, but the people have no money to buy **fertilizers** to make the soil better. If the crops do not grow,

DEVELOPED AND DEVELOPING COUNTRIES OF THE WORLD

people do not have enough money to buy food from elsewhere to feed their families.

The first part of this book looks at some of the projects that are helping the people of the developing countries to grow more food.

The richer countries of the world are called the developed countries. In the developed countries most people have plenty to eat. But what people

The countries coloured green are the developing countries of the world. The countries coloured blue are the richer, developed countries. The places named on this map are named in the book.

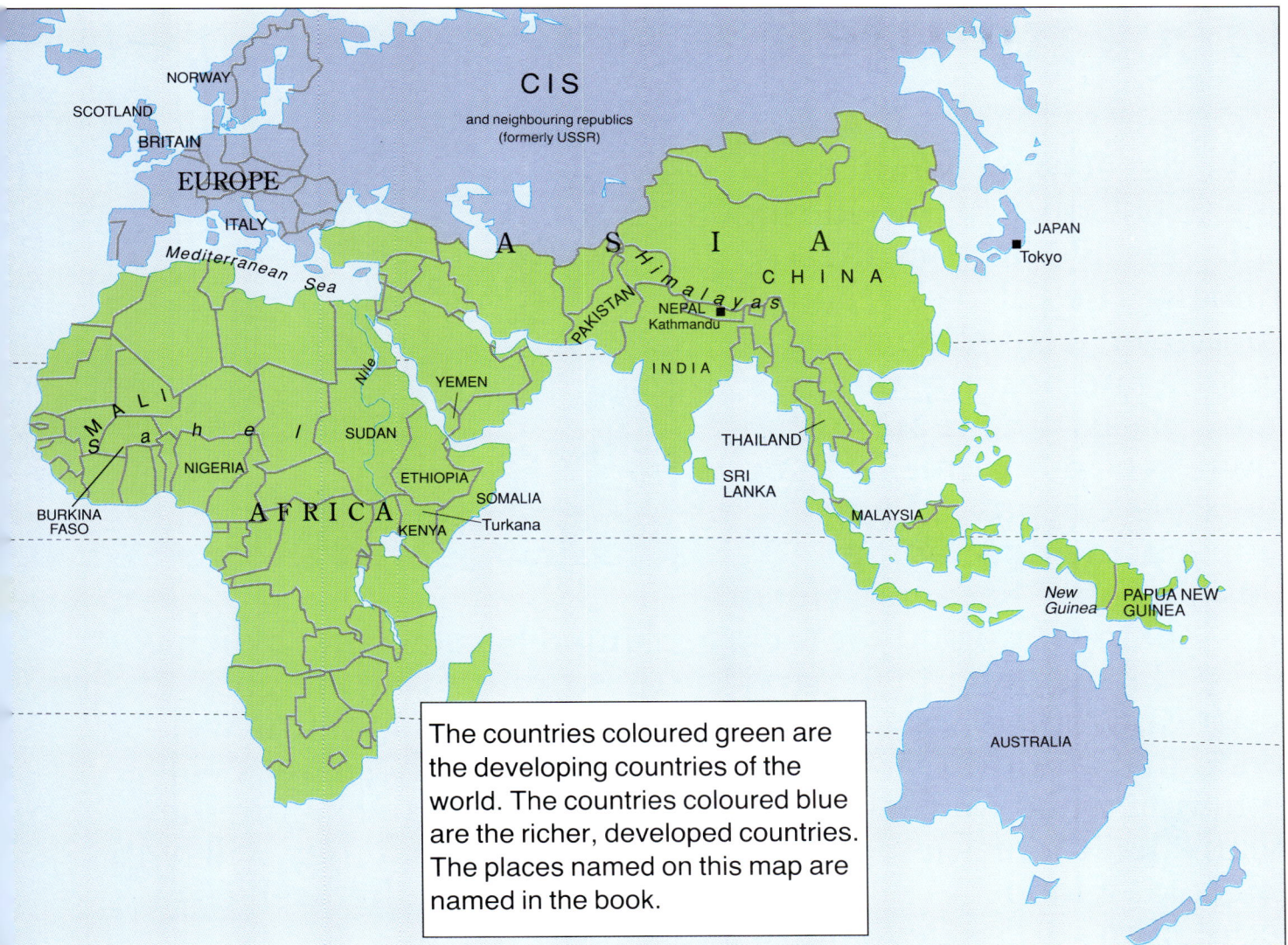

eat and the way the food is grown is always changing. The second part of this book looks at some of the new ways of growing food in the developed countries of the world.

Words in **dark** type are explained at the end of each section. There are also boxes called **Food for thought** with questions about food for you to think about.

famine – a serious shortage of food that causes many people to die.
fertilizers – substances that people put on to soil to make crops grow better.

Trees for life

In the developing countries people use trees to provide food for themselves and for their animals. They also use the wood from trees to burn for cooking and heating. But in many places people are cutting down trees more quickly than new trees can grow. Poor people in the developing countries have to spend a lot of time looking for wood for fuel. In the Himalayas, and in parts of Africa, women and children spend many hours every day gathering wood for fuel. This means that there is less time for cooking food. As the **populations** of the developing countries get larger, more people spend more time looking for fuelwood.

Planting trees

Now, some countries have started to plant trees to provide more food and fuel for the future. In Kenya in Africa, schoolchildren have helped to plant many trees in small tree nurseries. In Haiti, farmers have planted 25 million trees in only four years. Sometimes people plant trees that will grow quickly. Other trees are planted because they will have fruits or nuts that are good to eat, or wood that burns well.

Of course, these trees will take time to grow before they can be used. But they will help people to feed themselves in the future.

◁ Women collect wood for fuel in Africa.

▷ Children in Sri Lanka help to plant trees.

▷ People in China are planting forests to replace the trees cut down for farming.

◁ Cooking on an open fire in Nepal. Many people in poor countries cook on an open fire.

Forest farms

One of the best ways to use trees is to grow them together with crops. This is called **agroforestry**. The leaves that fall from the trees help to fertilize the soil. If there is a **drought**, crops will quickly die. But trees can live for longer without water, so farmers can still use the trees for food.

In Peru, farmers plant corn, rice, cassava and other crops. Around these crops they grow fruit and nut trees. For the first few years the farmers eat and sell their crops. Then they pick the fruits and nuts off the trees. After about 20 years the farmers cut the trees down. The wood is

◁ Agroforestry at work. Bean plants grow under banana trees.

A useful tree

The Indian neem is a very useful tree. Its seeds contain oils that can be used in soap and medicines. The seeds are also ground up to make a substance that protects grain against harmful insects.

▷ Young neem trees are protected by sticks to stop animals eating the green shoots.

used for cooking and heating.

Agroforestry is also being used in China to help people grow more food. In one place people have planted rubber trees further apart than usual. In-between the rubber trees they have put tea plants. The rubber trees grow well because the air can move around them easily. This stops diseases moving from one tree to another. The tea plants grow well in the shade of the rubber trees. So the two plants grow well together.

Food for thought
● How much time does your family spend each day buying, growing and preparing food?

population – the people that live in a country.
agroforestry – growing trees and crops together.
drought – a long period when little or no rain falls.

9

Water in the desert

Many countries of the world have to irrigate land in order to grow crops. Irrigation is when water is carried to fields through pipes or ditches. In India, Pakistan and China at least half of the food is grown on irrigated land. But in the deserts of northern Africa only a small amount of land is irrigated.

Gardens in the sand

The Tuareg people of northern Africa used to have a **nomadic** way of life. They moved from place to place with their cattle. But the cattle have died because of drought. Many Tuareg families now live in villages. They have started a new life by making gardens to grow crops. Water to irrigate the crops comes from small wells. The Tuareg have dug the wells at the edges of

Cleaning water

People living near the River Nile in Sudan have found a cheap way to clean up dirty river water for drinking. They take the seeds from the moringa tree and grind them up. They put the seeds in the water and the dirt in the water sticks to the bits of seed. The seeds sink to the bottom, leaving clean water on top.

◁ Farmers in Kenya use a camel to drag a scoop through a small lake. The scoop lifts sand and dirt out from the bottom of the lake. This means more water will collect in the lake next time it rains.

△ Lines of stones help to trap water in Burkina Faso.

▽ A wind pump in Kenya. A wind pump helps to pull water up from deep under the ground.

lakes that fill up during the rainy season. Each well waters four or more gardens.

Magic stones

People in Burkina Faso are using stones to help to irrigate their land. The farmers dig the stones out of the soil. Women and children carry the stones in baskets to the fields. They build the stones into lines along the fields. When it rains the water collects behind the stones and irrigates the land.

nomadic – belonging to a group of people that moves from place to place.

New ways with old plants

There are about 250,000 kinds of plants in the world. But people only use about 20 kinds as crop plants. One way to help people in the developing countries to grow more food is to find new crop plants. These plants must be able to grow in poor soil and in places where there is little rain. Plants that only grow in the wild today may be used as crop plants tomorrow.

Scientists can help in other ways. Inside the cells of all living things are genes. Genes control how things grow, what they look like, and so on. Scientists can now pick out certain genes and move them from one plant to another. Moving genes like this is called **genetic engineering**. Scientists have used genetic engineering to make wheat, maize and rice ripen more quickly. These improved plants also have a

▽ Apple and pear trees from other parts of the world could be grown on mountain farms such as this one in Nepal.

Plants with a future?

The winged bean is a useful plant because people can eat every part of the plant except for the stem. The winged bean grows in parts of Asia. But people in other places could grow it as well. Another plant that people could grow more widely is the buffalo gourd. It grows wild in America, but it could also be grown as a crop. It grows well in poor, dry soil.

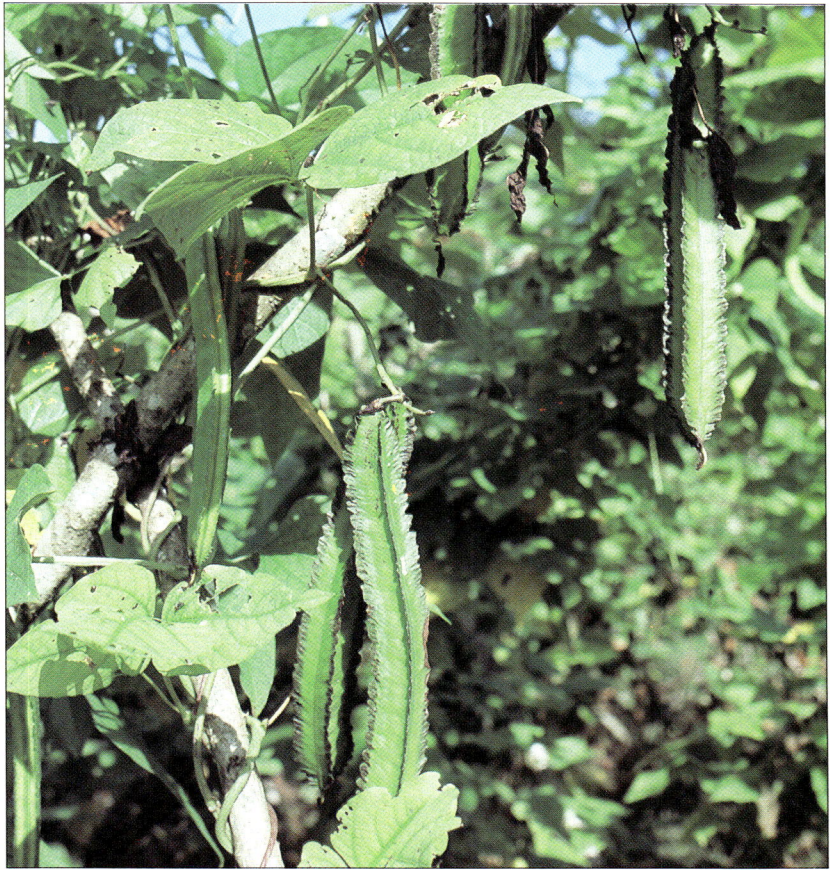

▷ Winged beans in Papua New Guinea

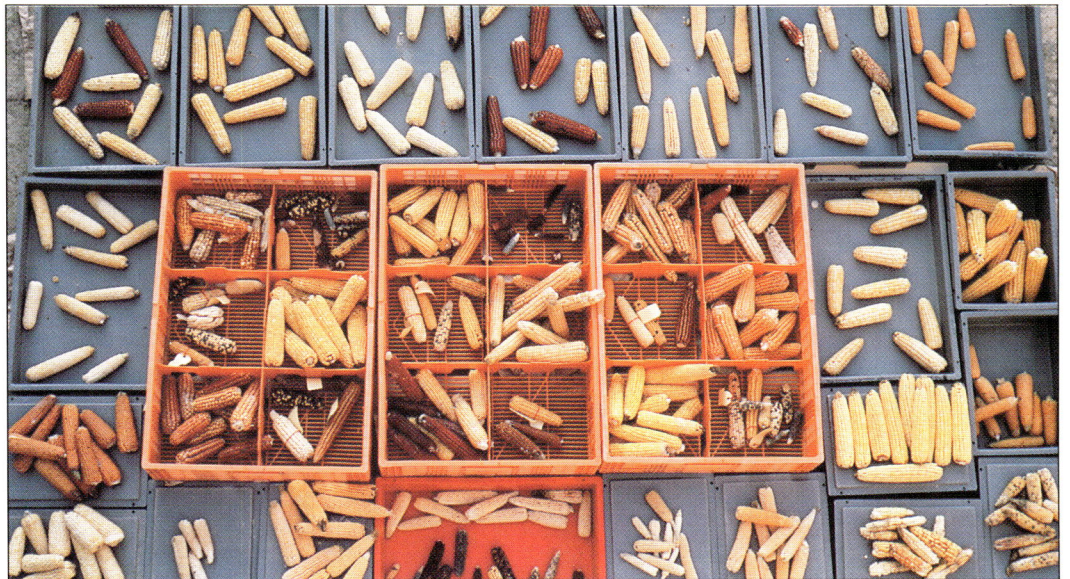

▷ Different kinds of maize produced by genetic engineering.

high **yield**. This means that people can get more food from each plant. Crops such as cassava, sorghum and millet that are grown in developing countries could be improved by genetic engineering too. For example, some plants die because the ground gets too hot. These plants could be changed so that they would not die.

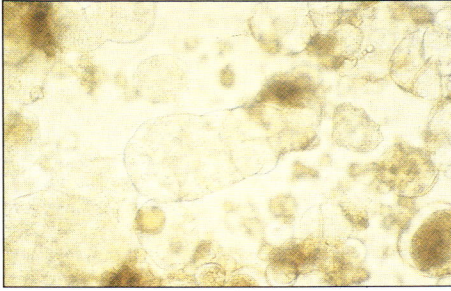

Copying plants

Scientists have found another way to produce more food. It is called **cloning**. The scientists put pieces of a plant into a special jelly. The pieces of plant feed on the jelly and grow to make many new plants. Hundreds of new plants can be made in this way.

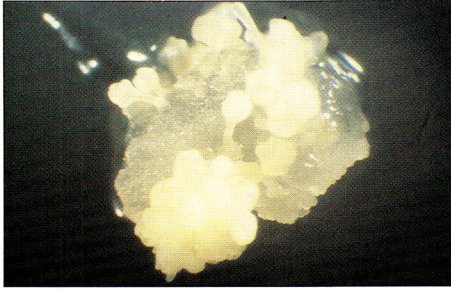

Added goodness

Some crops, such as cassava, do not contain much protein. Protein is one of the substances in food that people need to be healthy. People in Africa, Asia and Central and South America grow a lot of cassava.

△ Some of the stages of cloning a plant to make many new plants. Each new plant will look just like its original 'parent'.

△ Children carrying bread in Nigeria

Bread without wheat

Bread made from expensive imported wheat is popular in West Africa. Now scientists have worked out a way of adding a special gum to make bread from local crops such as maize, millet and cassava. Local farmers can grow the crops, and the bread is cheaper.

Now, scientists have found a special mould that adds more protein to dried cassava. The same thing could be done to make banana waste into a useful food for people.

◁ Bananas in a store in Costa Rica. In future, banana waste could be useful as a food for people.

genetic engineering – changing a plant or animal by adding or taking away certain genes.
yield – the amount of food such as grain or fruit produced by a plant.
cloning – making many plants or animals from one 'parent' plant or animal.

The useful camel

People have used camels for work and as food for thousands of years. Camels can carry people and pull ploughs. They can provide milk and meat. People use the wool from a camel to make cloth. They use the skin to make shoes, saddles and containers for water.

Camels can go for a long time without water. This means that they can live in very dry places where cattle and other animals would die. In a dry season a camel often drinks water only once a week.

Camel milk

In Africa, some of the boys who look after camels live only on camel's milk. Camel's milk is very white. It is full of goodness

▽ Moving home in Somalia. The camel is carrying this family's house and belongings.

△ A woman in Turkana,
Kenya, milking a camel.

and proteins. It is a better food for people
than milk from cows, sheep or buffalo. If
there is a drought and crops die, camel's
milk can provide enough food to keep
people alive.

Feeding camels

The animals that live in the desert feed off the plants that grow there. But in the dry desert sand not many plants can grow. Camels only eat part of a plant — they nibble it and then move on. This means that the plant can continue to grow. Other animals, such as sheep and goats, do more damage to the desert plants. They eat the whole of a plant.

People who own camels in the desert are usually nomadic. They move from one place to another because there are not enough plants in one place in the desert to feed their animals all the year round.

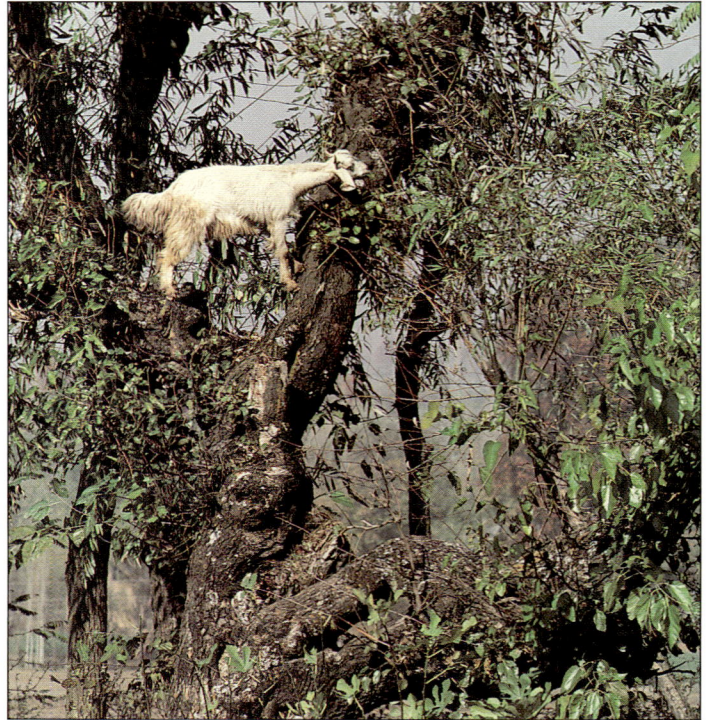

△ A goat will eat all the leaves that it can reach off a tree.

▽ Nomadic people on the move with their animals in Ethiopia

Sheep, goats and gaurs

Sheep and goats are sometimes kept in pens. Here people can look after them properly, and the animals produce more milk. People drink the milk, and use it to make butter, cheese and yoghurt.

There may be other animals living in the wild that could be useful to people in the future. In Malaysia, a kind of cow called a gaur lives in the forests. The gaur grows quickly. People are now starting to keep the gaur as a domestic animal.

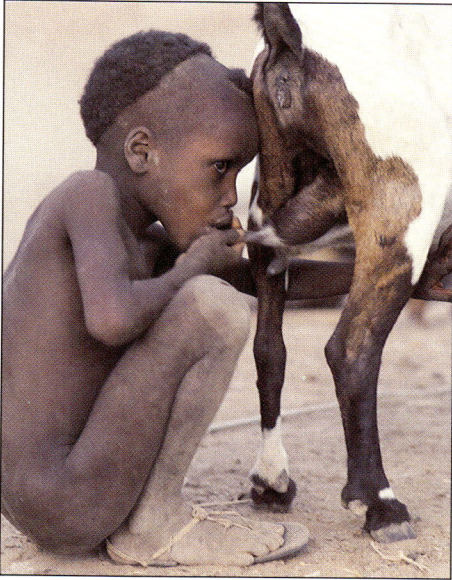

△ A boy in Turkana takes a drink from one of his goats.

▷ A gaur

Animal power

Women in developing countries spend hours every day grinding grain into flour. A machine would be faster, but machines are too expensive for most families. Now there is a kind of mill that is powered by a donkey, a horse or an ox. One mill can be shared by everyone in a village.

19

Farming the sea

Fish is a healthy food with lots of proteins and **vitamins**. Every year the catch of fish worldwide is about 92 million tonnes. Japan is the country that catches the most fish. It catches about 12 million tonnes every year.

As the number of people in the world gets bigger the sea can be used to provide extra food. There are more than 30,000 different kinds of fish. But people eat only a few hundred different kinds. Sometimes people do not want to try new kinds of fish. The Arctic Pollack was not popular when it was first caught. But now it is sold in sticks, coloured pink to look like crab meat, and people like it.

△ Arctic Pollack

▽ A salmon farm in Norway. (Inset) A fish farmer squeezes a male fish to fertilize female eggs.

Fish farms

In some places people keep fish in fish farms. There are fish farms for salmon in Scotland, Norway and other countries in Europe. People control the amount of food and light that the fish get. They also make sure the water is the right temperature for the fish to grow. When the fish are old enough they are put into cages floating in the sea. The fish live in the cages until they are big enough to be sold.

Shellfish

Shellfish can also be farmed by people. Mussels will grow on ropes or on netting floating in the seawater. Oysters will grow on plastic trays.

People in Europe and America are eating more and more prawns every year. There are many prawn farms in Asia. But the food for the prawns is difficult to catch, and it is expensive. Now scientists have made a special kind of food for prawns. This makes it easier to produce prawns in fish farms.

Another kind of shellfish is krill. A krill looks like a small shrimp. Krill live in the icy seas around the South Pole. Krill are full of proteins and vitamins. They could be used as food for people and animals in the future. Russia, Japan

△ Krill (top)
◁ Fishing for krill. The krill are put in a freezer on board the ship (above).

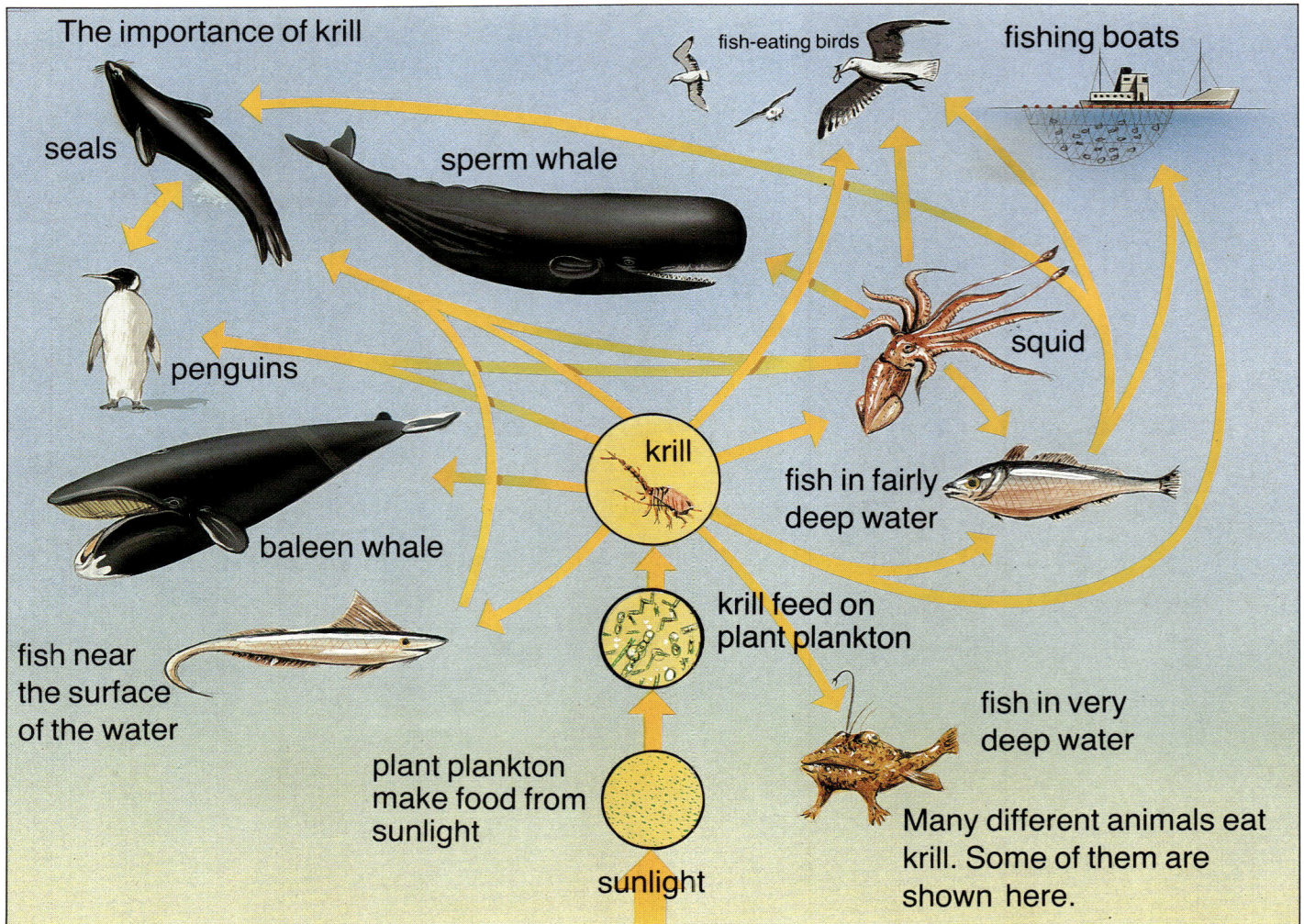

The importance of krill

seals

sperm whale

fish-eating birds

fishing boats

penguins

squid

baleen whale

krill

fish in fairly deep water

fish near the surface of the water

krill feed on plant plankton

fish in very deep water

plant plankton make food from sunlight

sunlight

Many different animals eat krill. Some of them are shown here.

and Norway already fish for krill. But there are many problems if other countries also want to start fishing for krill.

The first problem is that many animals in the sea eat krill. If people take too many krill out of the sea then there might not be enough left for the whales, fish, seals and penguins. Another problem is that the sea around the South Pole is frozen for most of the year. Fishing boats can only work for a few weeks in the summer, when the ice melts.

Despite these problems krill is already used in food for people. Krill can be made into fish fingers, sausages, and food for fish farms. Krill is likely to be an important food for people and animals in the future.

Vegetables from the sea

People in Japan use a lot of seaweed in their food. Seaweed is added to soups and sauces and eaten as a vegetable. There are many different kinds of seaweeds around the world. Many of these could be used as food in the future.

△ A ship collects seaweed off the coast of Norway.

▷ A seaweed farm in Japan

vitamins – substances in food that people need to keep them healthy. There are many different kinds of vitamin.

More food or less?

Today, many developed countries can produce most of the food they need. Farmers in these countries use chemical fertilizers and **pesticides** on their crops. The fertilizers make the crops grow better. The pesticides stop insects eating the crops. The farmers can also buy special animal food to keep their animals healthy.

But people are worried about the chemicals that are put on crops and used in food for animals. Some people think that the chemicals may not be healthy for humans. Many people are also worried about factory farming. This is when animals like pigs and hens are kept indoors in small spaces. They are not allowed to move around or go outside.

Organic farming

Many people are becoming interested in **organic farming** An organic farmer uses natural ways to produce fruit, vegetables and meat. No chemical fertilizers and pesticides are used on organic farms. Animals are allowed to move around outside. Organic farms need more people to work on them. This means that

◁ Spraying crops with pesticide

△ Pigs can be kept outdoors. The shelters are for bad weather.

◁ A female pig with her piglets

organic food is more expensive. But many people are happy to pay a bit more in order to eat healthier food.

▷ Hens in a battery cage

Room to move?

▬ Wing flaps

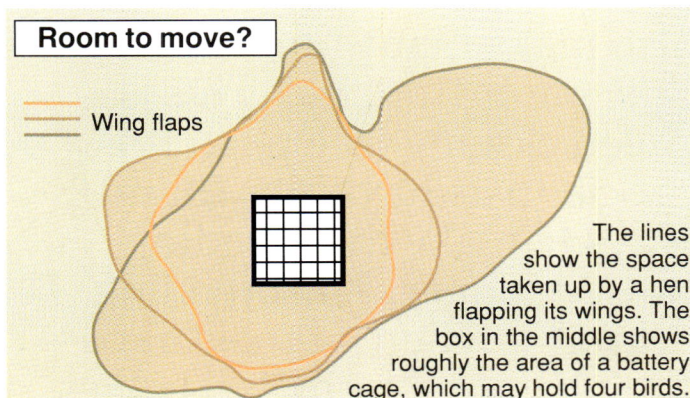

The lines show the space taken up by a hen flapping its wings. The box in the middle shows roughly the area of a battery cage, which may hold four birds.

More room to move

Most hens that lay eggs are kept in cages. The cages are in buildings which are called batteries. The amount of heat, light, water and food is carefully controlled. This is a good way to produce eggs. But it is not very kind to the hens. Three or four hens share a cage. There is not enough space for the hens to flap their wings or turn round.

Some farmers keep hens outside. This is called free-range farming. But it is more difficult for the farmers. It takes longer to check that the hens are healthy. Sometimes the hens attack each other. Free-range farming is also more expensive. So people have to pay more for their eggs.

◁ Cows being milked Should cows be given hormones to make them produce more milk?

More milk from cows

Hormones are chemicals that control how an animal's body works. Scientists can collect these hormones and use them to keep animals healthy. They can also use them to make beef cattle grow more quickly, but these hormones are banned in many countries. Another hormone makes dairy cattle produce more milk. But many people are worried that the hormone will still be in the milk when they drink it. People also ask why we need to produce more milk when there is already too much (see page 36).

Breeding animals

Until now, farmers have used their best animals for breeding. Now there is another, faster way to produce strong animals. Scientists can use genetic engineering (see page 12) to produce animals that will not catch diseases easily and that will grow quickly. Scientists can also make many animals from one 'parent' animal. This is called cloning (see page 14).

Scientists have also found ways to make the breeding season longer. The breeding season is when animals have their babies. Normally, babies

△ Most lambs are born in the spring.

are born at a certain time of year. For example, sheep have their lambs in spring. Now scientists can give the sheep a hormone that allows them to mate and produce lambs throughout the year, not just in the spring.

Food for thought
● Some people think that giving animals hormones to change the way they grow and breed is wrong. What do you think?

pesticides – chemicals sprayed on to crops to kill insects.
organic farming – farming without chemical fertilizers and pesticides.
hormones – chemicals in an animal's body that control how it works.

Amazing machines

The tractor is the most important machine on the farm. Today's tractors are very big and powerful. They can pull two or three machines at once. The farmer can do two or three jobs in a field at a time. He can turn the soil and sow the seeds in one go. This saves both time and money.

It is hard to imagine another machine ever doing all the jobs that a tractor does. But the gantry in the bottom picture on page 29 can do many things. The gantry can be used for planting and spraying crops as well as many other jobs. It is used in many countries from Australia to Israel.

Computer control
In the future, computers will be used to help the farmer.

Farmers already use computers to make sure that they are spraying the right amount of pesticide, or planting the right amount of seed. In the future, information from pictures taken from the air will be fed into the farmer's computer. This will help the farmer to plan what crops to plant and where to plant them.

△ Tractors of the future will have computers to help the farmer.

◁ A new tractor being tested. This tractor will be used in flooded rice fields.

◁ ▽ Collecting straw. This machine presses straw into small packs called wafers. The wafers can be used for bedding for animals, and for fuel.

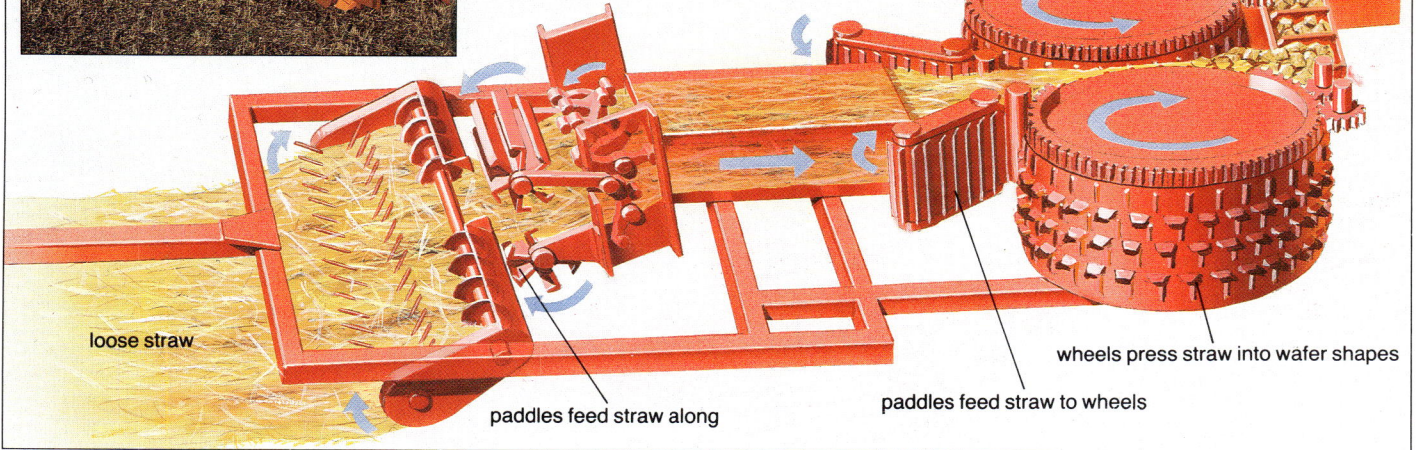

elevator lifts wafers into truck

loose straw

paddles feed straw along

paddles feed straw to wheels

wheels press straw into wafer shapes

▷ In America, one farmer has made a giant machine to suck insects off his strawberry plants. This means that he does not have to spray the strawberries with pesticides.

▽ The gantry can be used for planting, spraying and harvesting.

Man-made meat

When is a meat pie not a meat pie? Since the 1950s, some meat products such as mince, pies and stews have been made without using any meat. Soya beans are used instead. The soya beans are used to make a food called textured vegetable protein (TVP for short). To make TVP, the soya beans are ground to make a flour. Then the flour is made into strips and chunks which look and taste like meat.

Soya beans contain a lot of protein. They are easy to grow. TVP from soya could provide food for many people.

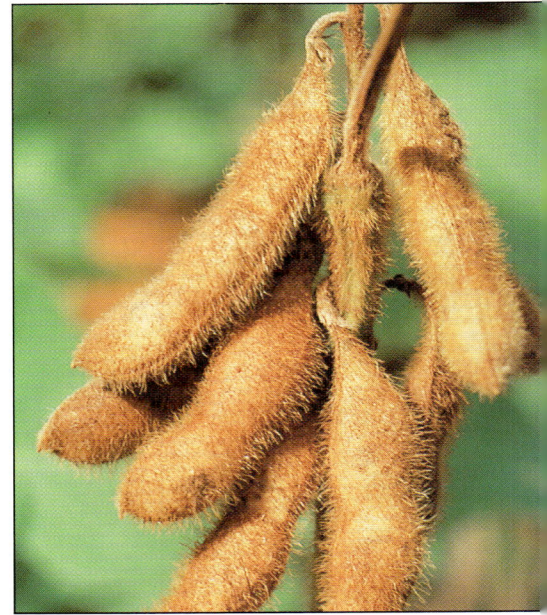

△ Soya beans

▽ Harvesting soya beans

◁ Some algae are grown in ponds and used to feed fish and shrimps.

Aquaculture – Aquaculture is when plants are grown in water. It is useful in places where the soil is very poor. Some of the plants that grow in water are called algae. Seaweeds are algae, and many tiny water plants are also algae. One kind of algae called *spirulina* is used in food for people. It is full of protein. More *spirulina* could be grown in the future.

◁ *Spirulina*

Fungus food

We already eat all kinds of **fungi**. The blue mould on cheese is a kind of fungus. Mushrooms are also fungi. There is a new food made from a tiny kind of fungus. This food is called myco-protein. The fungus grows in a container called a fermenter. Then it is dried. It is pale and has no taste, but it is chewy like meat. Colours and flavours are added to make the myco-protein look and taste like chicken, fish and many other foods. The first myco-protein products were sold in Britain in 1989.

Scientists can make other foods too. In the future, food factories could replace farms. In developing countries food factories could provide more food in places where it is difficult to grow crops.

Food for thought
- Have you tried any of the products described here? Why do you think they are made to look and taste like foods we already eat?

fungi – plants such as mushrooms or mould.

Keeping food fresh

In the past, people salted food to stop it going bad. Some foods were dried, smoked or pickled. In cold places, meat and fish were frozen in pits dug in the ice. We keep food in the same ways today. We use machines to smoke or pickle food. And we keep food in deep freezers and fridges to keep it fresh.

Most food that we buy in supermarkets contains **additives**. Some additives make the food last longer. Others add colour or taste to the food. In Britain about 2000 different additives are used in food. Most of them must be listed in the ingredients on the packaging of the food. In European Community countries some additives have an E number. This number can be used instead of the full name. The additives with the E numbers E200 to E299 are preservatives. They are used to make the food last longer.

Some people are worried about the use of additives in food. They think that additives may be bad for people's health.

Wrapped in plastic

Fruit and vegetables must stay fresh for several days. Plastic

△ These apples have been stored for four weeks. The apples in wrapping (left) have kept better than the apples on the right.

◁ This drum contains fruit that will be irradiated with radioactive rays.

wrappers can stop apples going yellow and stop mould growing on tomatoes. Bread is also wrapped in plastic. The plastic used for bread wrappers has holes in it to let water out. This stops the bread going soggy.

Using irradiation

Irradiation is a way of treating food so that it stays fresh. The food is treated with radioactive gamma rays. Fruit that is irradiated ripens more slowly and does not go mouldy. Irradiation destroys the **bacteria** in food that give people food poisoning. But irradiation also destroys some of the vitamins in food. Many people are worried about the effects of eating irradiated food. Irradiation is allowed in more than 30 countries. But some countries, such as Australia and Sweden, have banned it.

Food for thought
● Check the lists of ingredients on the food you eat. How many additives are used?

additives – substances that are added to foods.
bacteria – tiny plants that live in the air, water, soil and the bodies of animals.

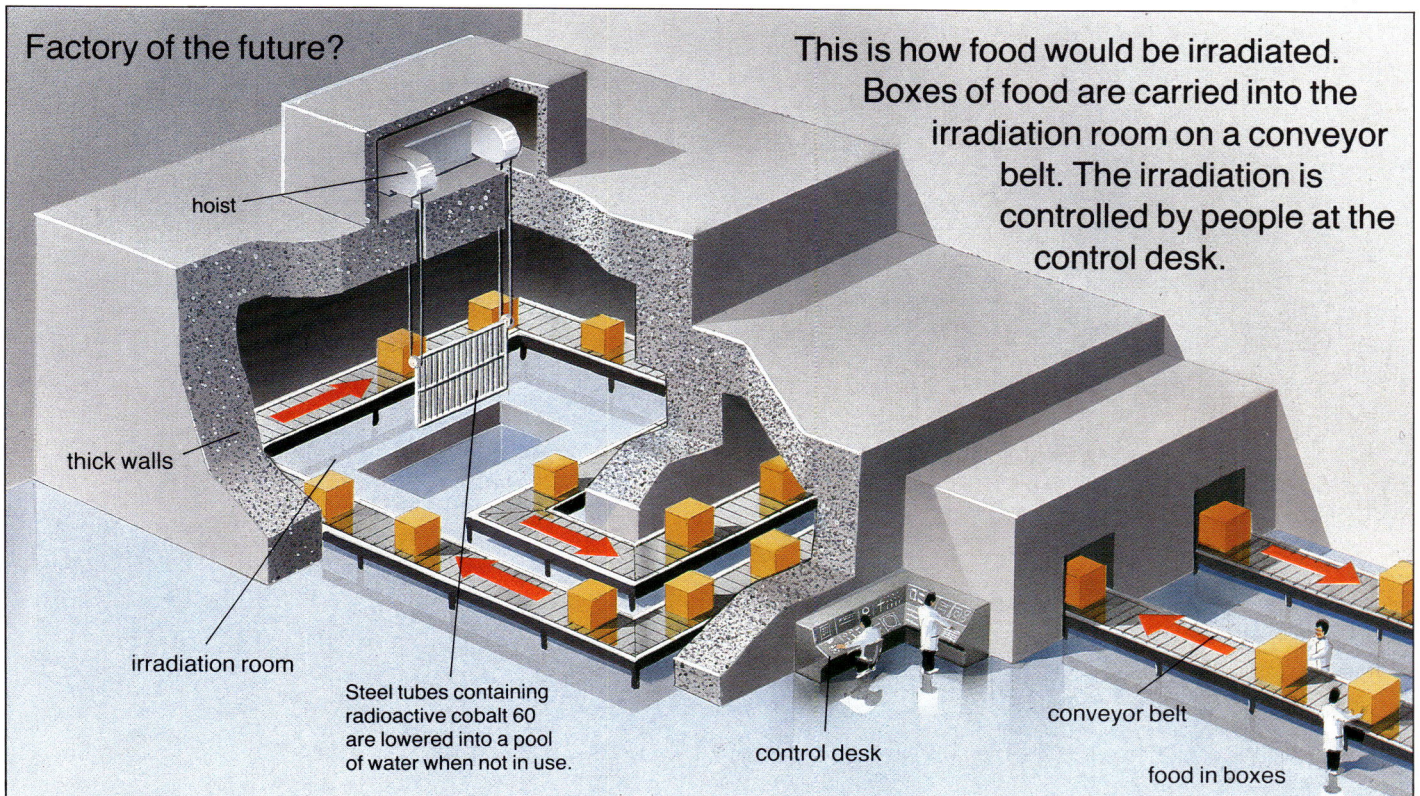

Factory of the future?

This is how food would be irradiated. Boxes of food are carried into the irradiation room on a conveyor belt. The irradiation is controlled by people at the control desk.

hoist

thick walls

irradiation room

Steel tubes containing radioactive cobalt 60 are lowered into a pool of water when not in use.

control desk

conveyor belt

food in boxes

Farms of the future

Crops that grow well in cooler **climates** will probably not grow in warmer places. So a farmer has to plant the right crops for the climate he lives in. But farmers all over the world will soon be affected by the **greenhouse effect**. The greenhouse effect is caused by pollution in the earth's atmosphere. As more pollution is trapped in the atmosphere of the earth the world is becoming warmer. Scientists think that the temperatures in many parts of the world could go up. You can see on the map below how much the temperature could rise in different areas of the world.

If the temperature goes up it will affect where crops are grown. You can see some

△ ▷ Maize and sunflowers (right) both grow well in a warm, dry climate.

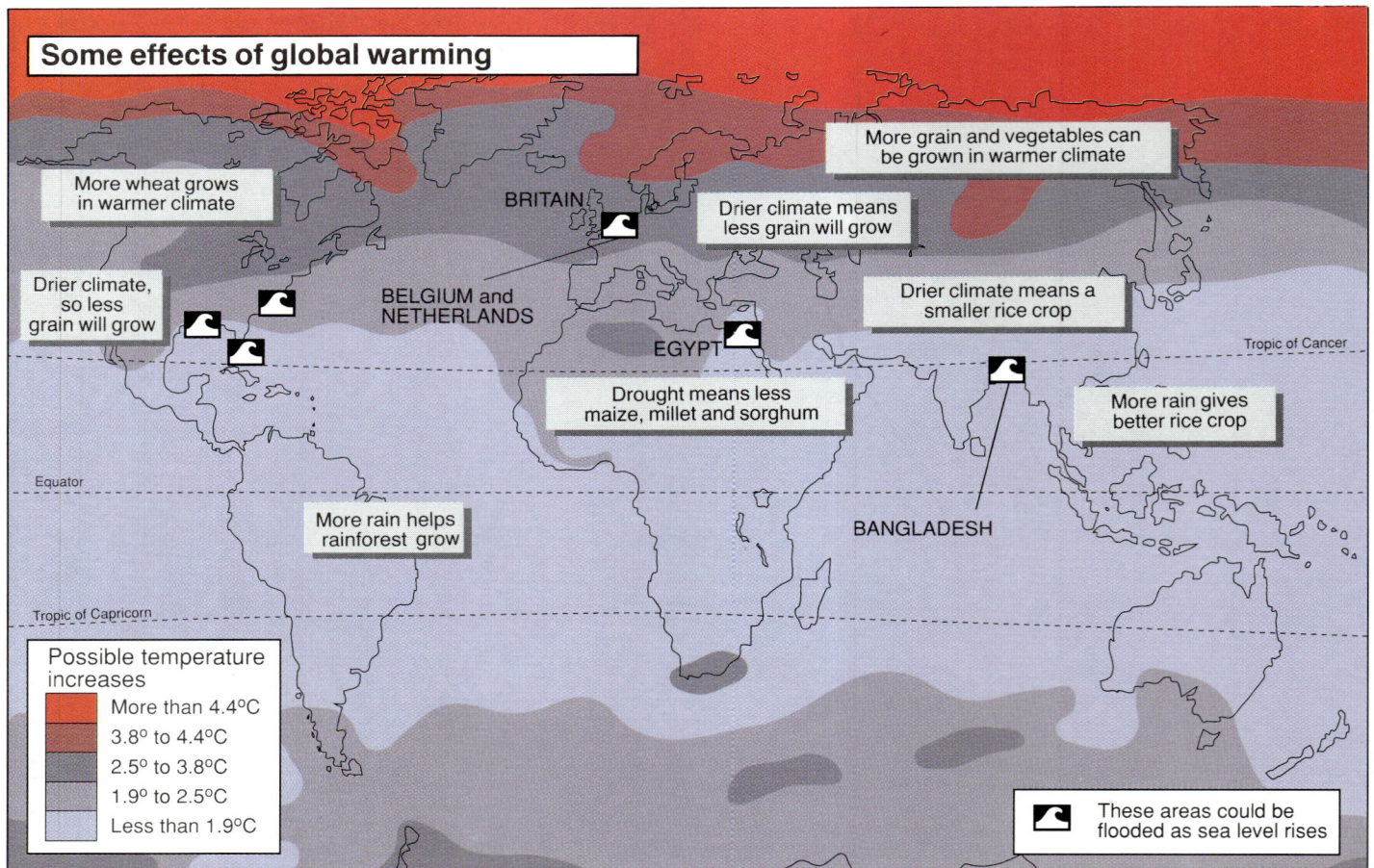

Some effects of global warming

More wheat grows in warmer climate

BRITAIN

More grain and vegetables can be grown in warmer climate

Drier climate means less grain will grow

Drier climate, so less grain will grow

BELGIUM and NETHERLANDS

Drier climate means a smaller rice crop

EGYPT

Tropic of Cancer

Drought means less maize, millet and sorghum

More rain gives better rice crop

Equator

More rain helps rainforest grow

BANGLADESH

Tropic of Capricorn

Possible temperature increases

- More than 4.4°C
- 3.8° to 4.4°C
- 2.5° to 3.8°C
- 1.9° to 2.5°C
- Less than 1.9°C

These areas could be flooded as sea level rises

of the changes on the map. The warmer temperatures would also make the ice caps at the North and South poles melt. This would make the sea level across the world rise. Many coasts would be flooded. These areas are also marked on the map.

Some scientists are thinking about ways of making use of the greenhouse effect. Many northern countries will have warmer and wetter climates. This means that

▽ Scientists plant different kinds of cereal in strips. They test the cereals to see how fast they grow and how easily they catch diseases.

farmers will be able to grow crops such as fruit and vegetables. They cannot grow these crops at present because the climate is too cold.

Producing too much food

In the developed countries of the European Community (EC) people produce more food than they can use. This is called a surplus. There are large stores of wheat, sugar, milk and wine that will go to waste. The EC is now trying to stop farmers producing too much food.

In Britain some farmers are using their land to keep sheep, goats or deer instead of growing crops. They are using these animals to produce wool, cheese and meat. Other farmers are planting trees on their land. Farmers could keep hens and pigs outdoors instead of inside

(see page 25). More land could be used for organic farming (see page 24).

In other places farmland could be sold and used for parks or golf courses. Some people think that more houses should be built on spare farmland. In the future, farmland in Europe could look very different.

Science in control

Scientists are helping farmers to make the most of the crops that they grow. Farmers can plant crops that are good for certain jobs. For example, using genetic engineering scientists have made some kinds of potatoes that are specially good for crisps, and some kinds of wheat that are specially good for bread. Scientists have also made a pesticide that does not

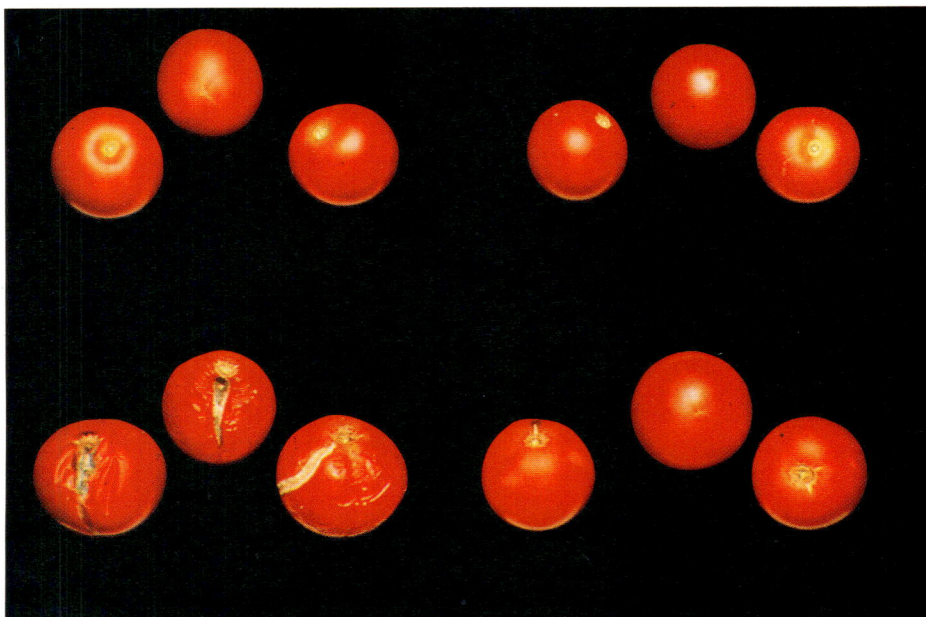

◁ Scientists have grown new kinds of tomatoes that will ripen without going soft or splitting.

use harmful chemicals. The pesticide is made from bacteria found in the soil. The pesticide is put on the seeds before the farmer plants them. The pesticide attacks any insect that tries to eat the plant.

New crops are always being tried out. Many people want to be able to buy more natural food, without chemicals and additives. Some fruits that grow wild in Britain are already used in other European countries. Sea buckthorn and rosehips are both full of vitamins. They could be grown and used for making jam and fruit juices.

▽ Sea buckthorn grows in the wild in Britain. It could be grown as a food crop.

Factory farms

Some farming is moving off the land and into factories. In factory farms plants are not grown in soil. Instead the plants grow on a special mat. The plants are given plant food to make them grow. This way of growing plants without soil is called **hydroponics**. Computers in the factory control the amount of light and the temperature in the building. There is no need to use pesticides or fertilizers. And there is no need to worry about the weather.

Growing vegetables by hydroponics uses less space and needs fewer people. Many other crops could be grown in this way in the future.

climate – the typical weather in an area over a long time.
greenhouse effect – the rise in temperature around the world caused by pollution in the atmosphere.
hydroponics – growing plants without soil, using liquid plant food.

▷ ▽ Lettuces (right) and spinach (below) can be grown using hydroponics.

38

Under glass in the desert

Imagine being shut in a giant greenhouse for two years. During that time you must grow all your own food. This is what has happened recently to eight scientists in Arizona, USA. They lived in a huge glass building in the desert. The building is called Biosphere II. The scientists were trying to find out more about the earth and its plant and animal life. They hope that the information they have got from living in Biosphere II will help them to set up stations in Space, or on other planets.

▽ A model of Biosphere II

△ Growing new plants

△ Ladybirds like to eat the insects that attack crops.

▷ Fish were kept in large tanks.

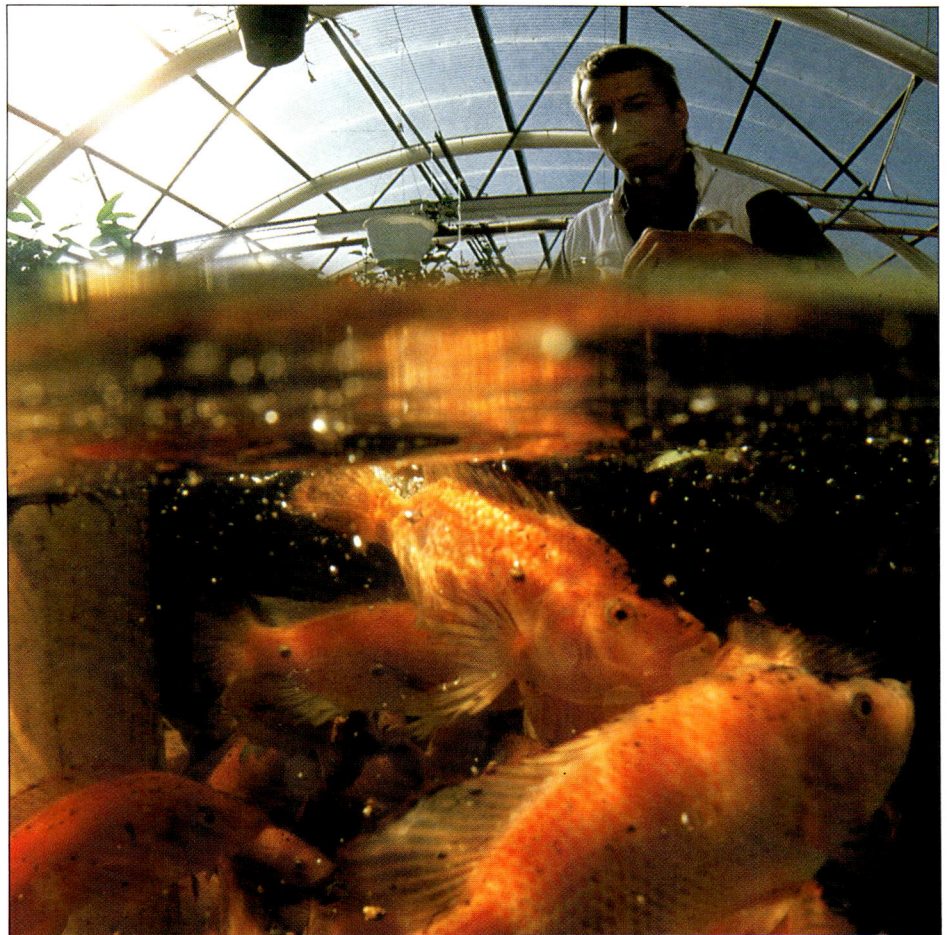

Home-grown food

The scientists grew about 150 different crops for food. They did not use pesticides on the crops. Instead they used insects such as ladybirds which like to eat the insects that destroy the crops. If any of the crops got diseases the scientists quickly grew new plants from tiny pieces of plants (see page 14). The scientist-farmers kept animals for milk and meat, as well as fish. They grew rice in the fish tanks too.

Food for thought
● What do you think it was like to live inside Biosphere II for two years? Would you have liked to live there?

Eating in Space

When the first people went into Space they ate liquid food squeezed out of tubes like toothpaste. The astronauts did not like this food very much because it was not very tasty. Since then, scientists have found ways to make Space food that is more like earth food. Today, astronauts on the Space **shuttle** have dinner on a special tray, and they eat with knives and forks.

But eating in Space is still not as simple as eating on earth. The tray is tied to the astronaut's leg to stop it floating away and

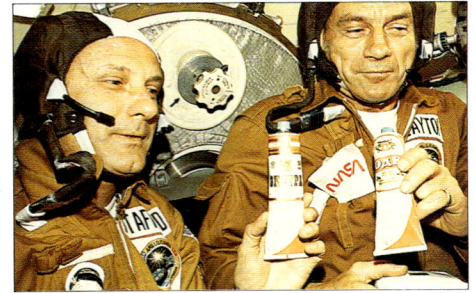

△ In the past space food came out of tubes.

△ Space food today is served on a tray.

◁ Eating on board the shuttle. The food tray is tied to the astronaut's leg.

42

the food in the tray is wrapped up. The astronauts must drink tea, coffee and other drinks through a straw.

Fresh food such as bread and fruit will only last for a few days in the Space shuttle because there is no fridge. So special food is made that will last for a long time without a fridge. The astronauts can heat up the food in the kitchen on the shuttle.

Living in Space

If people live in a Space station or on the Moon they will stay in Space for a long time. They will need to be able to grow their own fresh food. Scientists are looking at different ways of producing fresh food in Space. They could use hydroponics (see page 38) to grow crops. It may even be possible to grow some vegetables in the soil on the Moon.

Food for thought
● What food and drink would you take with you on a journey to Space? Plan a menu for a day.

shuttle – the American shuttle takes astronauts into Space.

A menu for a day

This is a menu for an astronaut for one day on board the Space shuttle. Each astronaut has food packages marked with a different coloured dot.

Menu

Breakfast
Orange drink
Cornflakes
Dried apricots
Scrambled eggs
Cocoa

Lunch
Tuna
Bread
Lemon pudding
Shortbread
Almonds
Apple drink

Dinner
Chicken and rice
Asparagus
Chocolate pudding
Grape drink

Snack
Butter biscuits
and coffee

Glossary

agroforestry – growing trees and crops together.

cloning – making many plants or animals from one 'parent' plant or animal.

drought – a long period when little or no rain falls.

famine – a shortage of food that causes many people to die.

fertilizers – substances that people put on soil to make crops grow better.

genetic engineering – changing a plant or animal by adding or taking away genes.

hormones – chemicals that control how an animal's body works.

hydroponics – a way of growing plants without using soil.

mould – a grey or green soft fungus that grows on damp walls or old bread.

nomadic – belonging to a group of people that moves from place to place.

organic farming – farming without the use of chemical fertilizers or pesticides.

pesticides – substances that kill insects which destroy crops.

yield – the amount of food such as grain or fruit produced by a plant.

Index

WEATHER

Richard and Louise Spilsbury

Evans

TITLES IN THE SCIENCE IN FOCUS SERIES:
DIGITAL TECHNOLOGY   THE EARTH'S RESOURCES   GENETICS
THE HUMAN BODY   THE SOLAR SYSTEM   WEATHER

Produced for Evans Brothers Limited by
Monkey Puzzle Media Limited
Gissing's Farm, Fressingfield
Suffolk IP21 5SH, UK

Published by Evans Brothers Limited
2A Portman Mansions
Chiltern Street
London W1U 6NR

First published 2006
© copyright Evans Brothers 2006

British Library Cataloguing in Publication Data
Spilsbury, Richard, 1963–
Weather. – (Science in focus)
1.Weather– Juvenile literature
I.Title II.Spilsbury, Louise
551.6

ISBN 0 237 52723 5
13-digit ISBN (from 1 January 2007) 978 0 237 52723 5

Editor: Clare Weaver
Designer: Jane Hawkins
Picture researchers: Sally Cole and Lynda Lines
Artwork by Michael Posen

Picture acknowledgements:
Action Plus 14; Alamy 10 (B&C Alexander); Corbis 20 (Issei Kato/Reuters), 24 (Tim Davis), 29 (Jim
Sugar), 39 right (Patrick Robert/Sygma); Getty Images front cover main image, front cover centre left,
6 (Beth Wald), 13 top (Pal Hermansen), 15 bottom (Steffen Thalemann), 17, 23 (Sean Gallup), 27
(AFP), 31 (Flip Nicklin), 38 (Oliver Strewe); NASA front cover top left, 8 bottom, 13 bottom, 39 left;
NHPA 8 top (Kevin Schafer); Rex Features 11 (Marco Simoni), 25 (Sunset), 41 (Michael Friedel);
Robert Harding Picture Library 30 top (Gavin Hellier); Science Photo Library 12 (T Van Sant/
Geosphere Project, Santa Monica), 15 top (Pekka Parviainen), 21 top (Kenneth Libbrecht), 30 bottom
(George Post), 32 (NASA), 35 (Mark Burnett), 36 (Hank Morgan), 40 (Jeremy Walker); Still Pictures 3
(Kent Wood), 16 (Kevin Schafer), 18 (SJ Krasemann), 22 (Kent Wood), 26 (Wim van Capellen), 33
(Weatherstock), 34 (Luiz C Marigo); Topfoto.co.uk 28.

VISIT OUR WEBSITE
Evans
www.evansbooks.co.uk

CONTENTS

WEATHER

The weather plays an important role in all our lives. It influences many aspects of daily life – from the food we eat and clothes we wear, to the places we choose to go on holiday and even the way we feel.

WHAT IS WEATHER?

The weather is the condition of the atmosphere around the Earth at a particular time and place. (The atmosphere is the blanket of gases that surrounds the Earth.) The weather determines whether it is hot or cold, wet or dry, sunny or grey outside. Other weather events include wind, storms, rain, sleet, hail and snow. In most places, weather can change from hour-to-hour, day-to-day, and season-to-season: one day it might be raining, the next it could be sunny.

CLIMATE

The climate of a place describes the annual weather patterns that have existed there for a long period of time. A country's climate tells you how hot, cold or wet it is likely to be there at certain times of the year. For example, Australia has a generally hot, dry climate, whereas Scotland has a cool, wet climate.

▼ Before most people dress in the morning, they look out of the window to see what the weather is like.

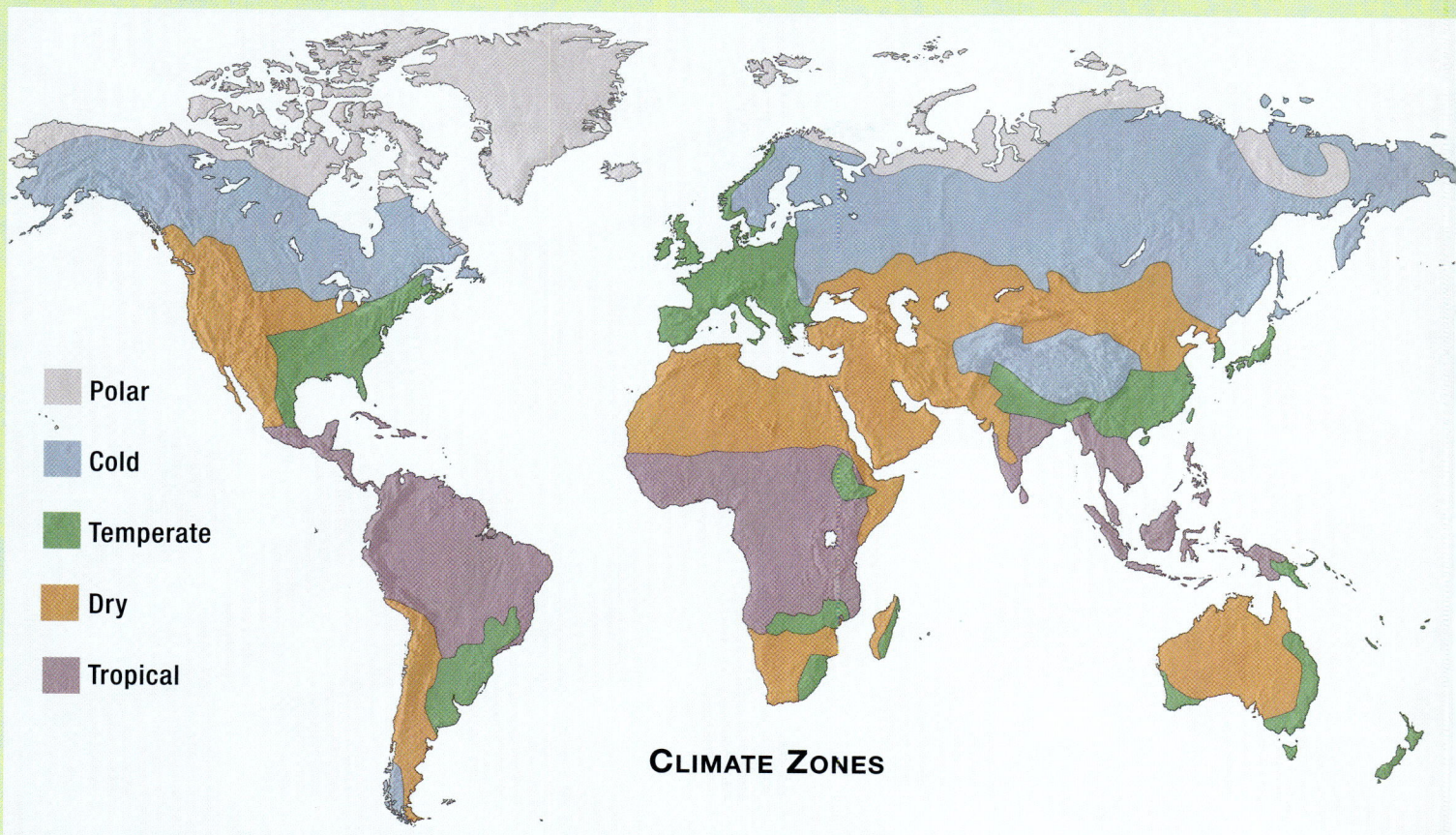

CLIMATE ZONES

Polar

Cold

Temperate

Dry

Tropical

▲ The five major climate zones across the Earth.

Scientists split the world into five major climate zones. Tropical climates have high temperatures all year round and get a large amount of rain. Dry climates have very little rain and are hot most of the year. Temperate climates have warm, dry summers and cool, wet winters. Cold climates are found in places that don't get large amounts of rain and where it gets very cold in winter. Places with polar climates have freezing temperatures for most of the year.

THE IMPORTANCE OF WEATHER

Weather has a huge impact on our lives. We often feel happiest in bright, sunny weather. For farmers, a slight drop in air temperature can lead to frosts that may damage crops. There's no point going on a skiing holiday if there's no snow! In many places, the weather influences the homes people live in. For example, in some snowy places buildings are constructed with steep sloping roofs, so the snow slides off them. Advance warning of extreme weather – for example, the forecast of a hurricane – can save lives.

FACT FOCUS

BIOMES

Biomes are large regions with very similar plant life. The main reason there are different biomes across the world is climate. For example, in areas with a very hot, dry climate, desert biomes form. With little rain, the land in deserts is dry and lacks nutrients. Desert plants and animals have special features that enable them to live there. Cactus plants survive by storing water in their stems, and many desert animals live underground during the day to escape the fierce heat.

THE SUN'S RAYS

The Sun is the nearest star to Earth. Its powerful rays light up and warm our planet. This warmth powers the world's weather.

RADIATION

Energy in the Sun's rays takes just 8 minutes to travel 150 million kilometres to Earth. This energy comes in the form of waves called radiation. The Sun produces three different kinds of radiation that reach Earth in significant amounts. Sunlight is the radiation that we can see, but ultraviolet (UV) rays and infrared rays are invisible.

▼ The Sun is an immense ball of superheated gases such as hydrogen. Its surface temperature is over 500 times the temperature of boiling water.

▲ Warm air rises because it is less dense than cold air. Birds such as condors use rising warm air called thermals to soar. Thermals provide lift without the effort of flapping wings.

A special layer of air in the atmosphere, called the ozone layer, soaks up most of the Sun's UV rays. However, some of this radiation gets through to the Earth's surface even if there is cloud cover in the sky. Ultraviolet rays can damage our skin and, in some cases, cause cancer. The heat we feel in the Sun is infrared radiation. It is this radiation that warms our world.

TRAPPING AND TRANSFERRING HEAT

Infrared radiation travels through the atmosphere and hits the Earth's surface. The land and sea absorb the heat and the warm surface then raises the temperature of the air above it.

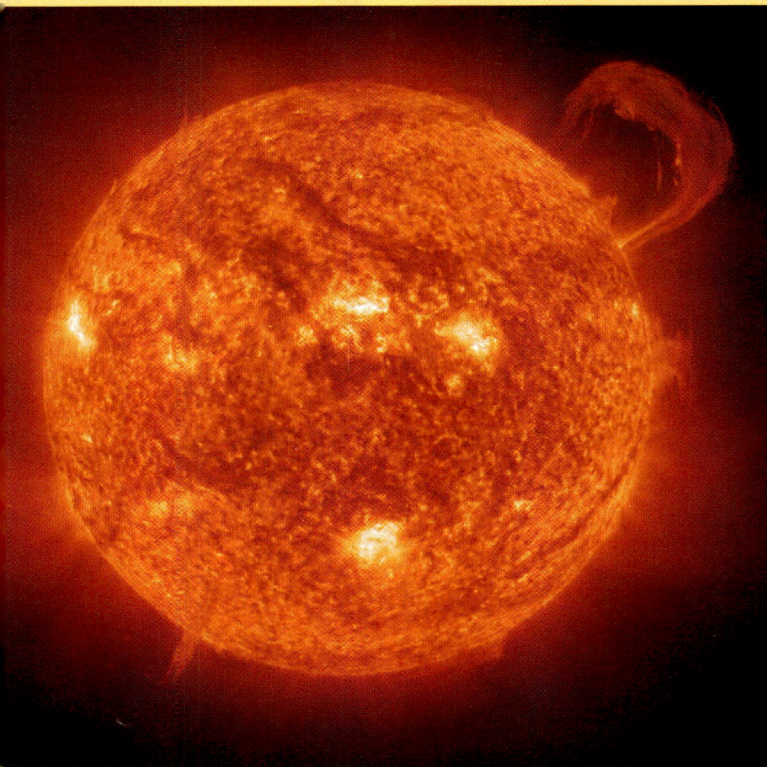

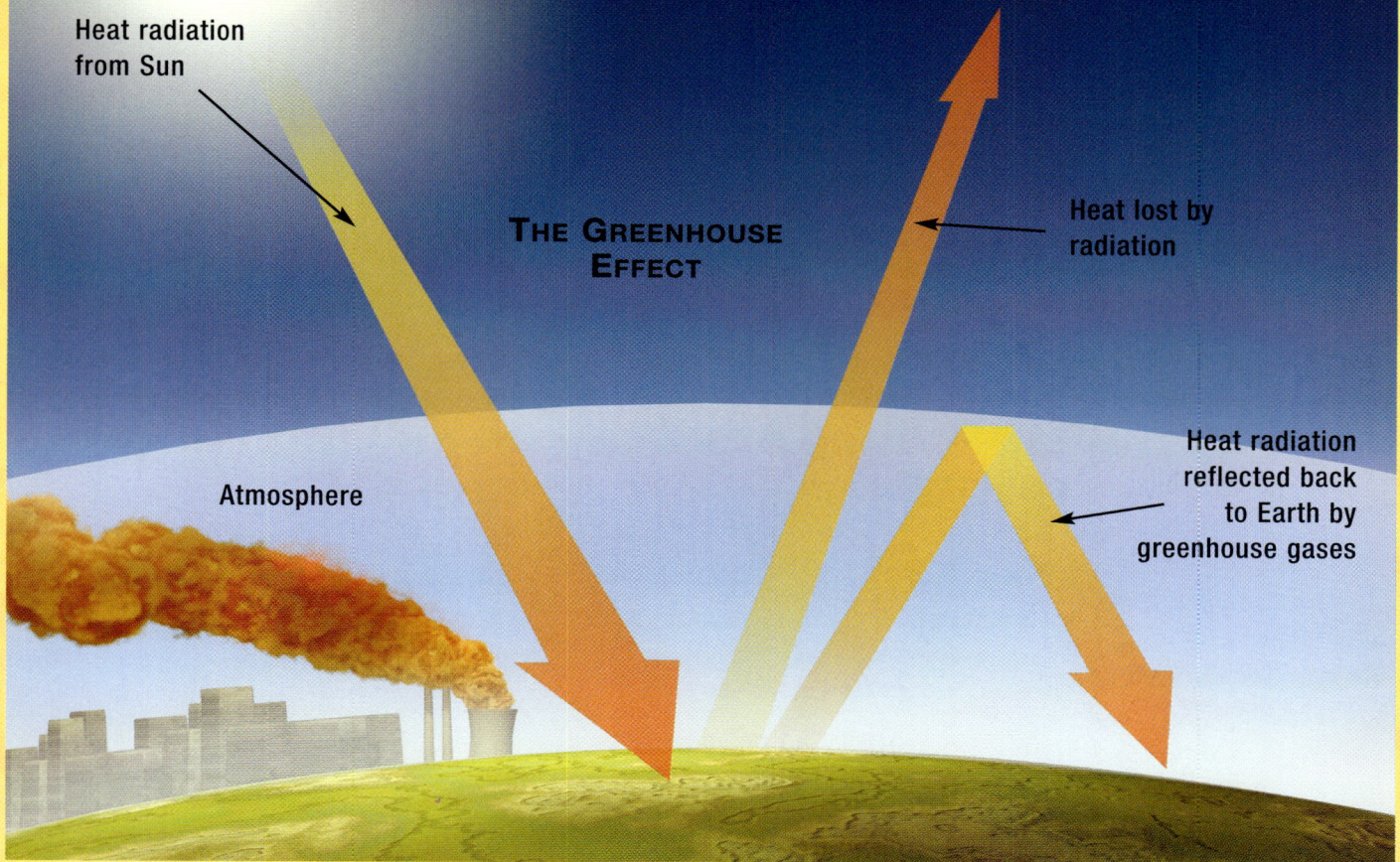

Heat radiation from Sun

THE GREENHOUSE EFFECT

Heat lost by radiation

Atmosphere

Heat radiation reflected back to Earth by greenhouse gases

Warm air is lighter than cold air and so rises above it. This temperature difference creates air movement and the transfer of heat energy between water, air and land. In turn, this causes different kinds of weather on Earth.

Some warm air rises so far its heat escapes into space, but most is trapped close to the Earth by gases, such as carbon dioxide, in its atmosphere. This is the greenhouse effect. By holding onto some of the heat it lets in, the atmosphere behaves a little like the glass in a greenhouse. The greenhouse effect is what keeps our planet warm enough to sustain life.

INSIDE LIGHT

Sunlight looks white, but it actually contains a mixture of different coloured light called a spectrum. The spectrum is visible as separate colours when white light shines through a prism. A prism is a wedge-shaped glass object that breaks light into its separate colours or spectrum. We see a rainbow when raindrops in the sky act as prisms and split sunlight.

All the dust and tiny droplets of water in the atmosphere also act as tiny prisms. They bend and reflect the spectrum colours. Blue and

▲ Without the greenhouse gases in the atmosphere, heat would escape back into space and Earth's average temperature would be about 35ºC colder than the current average of 15ºC.

violet are scattered more widely by these particles than red and orange. We see the cloudless sky as blue because lots of blue light is bending towards our eyes.

EVIDENCE FOCUS

CREATING RAINBOWS

Choose a sunny day to try this experiment. Put a small mirror at an angle, sticking out of a shallow bowl of water. Warmth from the sunlight causes water droplets to evaporate from the surface of the bowl. When light shines through the droplets, they split the light into a spectrum. You can see the rainbow colours best by reflecting the split light onto a sheet of white paper, held above the mirror.

TEMPERATURE DIFFERENCES

Some places on Earth are as cold as a freezer. In some areas, the ground gets so hot you can cook an egg on it! These temperature differences are caused by the amount of sunlight a place gets and by its geography.

TEMPERATURES AROUND THE EARTH

The main reason for temperature differences across the Earth is the curved surface of our spherical (round) planet. The Sun's rays travel to Earth in straight lines, but strike it at different angles in different places. At the Equator, the rays hit straight on, so the heat is concentrated, making this area very hot. At the North and South Poles, the coldest places on Earth, the rays strike the Earth's surface at a slanting angle. That means the warmth gets spread out over a very wide area.

TEMPERATURE, DAYS AND SEASONS

Another major factor affecting temperature is the movement of the Earth relative to the Sun. Each day, the Earth spins one complete turn on its axis, an imaginary line that goes through the Earth's core from pole to pole. The North and South poles are the two extreme points at the ends of the Earth.

▼ In the Arctic, close to the North Pole, winter months are dark and cold because of the tilt of the Earth away from the Sun.

The places facing, or nearest, the Sun are warmer and get more sunlight than those facing away from it. So, day is warmer than night. This difference is enhanced in deserts, where there are rarely any clouds to provide shade by day, or trap heat by night, so temperatures range from baking to near freezing.

Seasons happen because the Earth is tilted at an angle along its axis. As it orbits (travels around) the Sun through a year, the part of the Earth facing the Sun changes. For example, spring and summer happen in March to September in the northern hemisphere (the half of the Earth north of the Equator), but from September to March in the southern hemisphere (the half of the Earth south of the Equator).

THE LIE OF THE LAND

The characteristics of the Earth's surface also affect the temperature of a particular place. As altitude (height above sea level) increases, the air temperature falls because the air gets less dense and cannot heat up. That's why mountaintops are cold even in hot countries. Aspect is also important. In the northern hemisphere, slopes facing south get more direct sunlight than north-facing slopes, so they are warmer.

Distance from the sea plays a part in temperature, too. Coastal places are usually warmer than areas inland during the winter,

▲ Many houses in hot parts of the world are painted lighter colours to reflect infrared radiation and stay cooler inside.

because the sea cools down more slowly than land. A final factor affecting temperature is the albedo effect. This is the way different surfaces reflect different amounts of light and heat. For example, ploughed fields are dark. They reflect a low amount of heat and light, but they absorb much of it, so they stay much warmer than lighter surfaces, such as icebergs.

HISTORY FOCUS

BENJAMIN FRANKLIN (1706–1790)

Franklin was a printer, scientist, musician, politician and inventor in America. He carried out many important experiments – on electricity, for example – and invented the lightning conductor. In 1729, he examined the albedo effect by laying different coloured pieces of cloth on top of snow. He found that the darkest cloth melted snow beneath it, and sank, because it absorbed heat from sunlight. The lightest cloth did not sink because it reflected sunlight away.

ATMOSPHERE AND PRESSURE

The atmosphere is the blanket of gases that surrounds the Earth. It extends over 560 kilometres above the surface of the planet. Weather happens in the layer of atmosphere closest to Earth.

▲ Our planet is separated from the black space around it by the gas-filled atmosphere.

AIR IN THE ATMOSPHERE

The atmosphere absorbs some of the intense heat given off by the Sun, and thus makes it possible for us all to live in our world without being burned up during the day or freezing during the night. The air in the atmosphere is made up of different gases: 78 per cent nitrogen, 21 per cent oxygen, 0.9 per cent argon, 0.03 per cent carbon dioxide, and trace amounts of other gases, including water vapour (water that has evaporated into a gas in the air). The gases in the atmosphere are held in place by gravity.

AIR PRESSURE

The weight of the air in the atmosphere presses down on the Earth. At sea level on Earth, each square metre (m^2) has 10 tonnes of air above it. As you get higher above sea level, air pressure falls, because there is less air above you. Usually, you cannot feel this air pressure, because air within your body pushes out, counteracting the pressure of the air outside. However, at high altitudes (the height above sea level), the thinner air makes it more difficult to breathe.

Air pressure also varies over time, and from place to place. For example, there is always an area of high pressure over the North and South Poles, and an area of low pressure over the Equator. Changes in air pressure bring changes in the weather and make winds blow.

EVIDENCE FOCUS

PROVE AIR HAS WEIGHT

- Tie a piece of string around the middle of a stick, or piece of cane, until it balances.

- Tie an empty balloon to one end and a blown-up balloon to the other.

- The full balloon should pull down, because air inside it makes it heavier than the empty one.

▶ These patterns of multi-coloured light are called aurora borealis. They happen in some places above Earth when atomic particles from the Sun collide with atoms in the thermosphere (see below).

LAYERS OF ATMOSPHERE

The Earth's weather all happens in the lowest layer of the atmosphere – the troposphere, which extends to around 16 kilometres above the Earth. The troposphere contains 90 per cent of the air in the atmosphere and most of the water vapour.

The stratosphere is the next layer up. It contains the ozone layer, but it has little water vapour, the air is thinner, and the temperature rarely goes above 0°C. In the mesosphere, temperatures drop to −93°C as you increase in altitude, but in the thermosphere the temperature rises as it is closer to the Sun. The exosphere, starting 483 kilometres above Earth, has so little air it is virtually part of space.

◀ Without air, there is zero pressure on things in space. Astronauts wear pressurised spacesuits to stop their bodies swelling.

WATER IN THE ATMOSPHERE

The water vapour in the atmosphere is the key to many kinds of weather. Without this moisture, there would be no clouds, rain, sleet or snow, thunder and lightning, or fog.

HOW DOES WATER VAPOUR GET THERE?

When heat energy from the Sun warms water on the surface of puddles, ponds, lakes, reservoirs and oceans, some of that water evaporates.

EVIDENCE FOCUS

EVAPORATION ENERGY

It takes a transfer of energy for materials such as water to change state – from a liquid to a gas, for example. You get cool rapidly after exercising outside because liquid sweat evaporates. This happens when heat energy from your body is transferred to movement energy in water (sweat) particles as they change to water vapour.

▲ When you are hot and sweaty, the water from your body evaporates into water vapour to become part of the humidity in the air.

Heat energy makes the molecules within water move faster and faster, and jostle against each other. Some molecules break free and escape into the air as water vapour. Every day, 1,000 billion tonnes of water evaporate from the oceans alone, and end up in the air.

HUMIDITY

Humidity is the amount of water in the air. The air just above the ground always contains the most moisture. This is because the warmer the air is, the more water vapour it can hold, and the air nearer ground level is usually warmer than that above it. Warm air at 30°C can hold three times more water vapour than cold air at 10°C. This is because water condenses when it is cold. It starts to change from a gas back into a liquid state.

FOG, DEW AND FROST

At night, the Sun is on the opposite side of the Earth. Warmth absorbed by land during the day starts to escape into the atmosphere. Fog forms late at night, early in the morning, or when the air has cooled to a point at which the water vapour in it can no longer be held and begins to change into droplets. The change of state from a gas to a liquid when the gas cools is called condensation.

Dew and frost form in a similar way. On nights when the air is still and the skies are clear, warmth from the land escapes faster than usual. The air close to the ground cools down so rapidly that it actually becomes cooler than the air above it. This is called a temperature inversion. The low-lying moisture in the air condenses into water droplets that collect on plants to form

▼ Sea fog forms when moist air that has been lying over a warm area of water blows over colder water, cools and condenses.

dew. On very cold nights, when the water vapour comes into contact with very cold surfaces, it condenses and forms ice, instead of water droplets, to create frost.

▼ Frost often forms on windows because warm air, which holds a lot of moisture, rapidly cools, condenses and freezes when it hits cold glass. As more water molecules freeze, ice sometimes forms distinctive patterns like leaves.

CLOUDS

If you have ever seen an image of Earth taken from space, the planet was probably partially hidden by a patchwork of white clouds. Clouds form in different ways, and in different places, around the world.

WHAT ARE CLOUDS?

Clouds are made up of microscopic droplets of water or crystals of ice. They appear in the air when invisible water vapour in the air condenses into visible water or ice. Dew point is the name for the point at which water vapour turns into droplets of water. However, if the air temperature is very cold – below 0°C – then water vapour can change straight into solid ice crystals. This process is called sublimation.

▼ Moist air is forced to cool rapidly when it is blown up a mountain. That is why clouds form and weather changes quickly at high altitudes.

In the atmosphere, condensation and sublimation happen most often on the surfaces of tiny, cold particles, such as smoke, dust and salt, which float in the air. In places where the air is exceptionally clean, condensation does not happen and clouds cannot form so easily.

CLOUD FORMATION

Clouds form when warm air rises. This happens when a band of heavy, cold air pushes beneath lighter, warm air. It happens when wind blows warm air up the side of a tall mountain. It also happens when warm land or ocean waters warm the air just above them.

A large bubble of warm air rises rather like a hot air balloon. As it moves higher into the atmosphere it cools. When the top of the bubble cools below the dew point, water droplets or ice crystals start to fill out a cloud. The cloud starts to look darker, because less sunlight can shine through it.

INVERSION CLOUDS

Sometimes, rising bubbles of cool, moist air that are near their dew point form low, sheet-like clouds. The bubbles cannot rise far into the troposphere because of temperature inversion. Inversions often happen on very warm days after cold nights, especially where cold air collects in valleys.

FACT FOCUS

CLOUD FORMATION

The clouds above Earth only form in the troposphere. This is because above that the air is too cold for much water vapour to be absorbed by air. Airplanes fly above the troposphere because there is less turbulence (rough, unstable air). Turbulence is caused partly by the movement of air as clouds form.

▼ Airplanes' hot engines release exhaust fumes full of water vapour into the air as they fly. These sublimate into streams of ice crystals that we call con trails or vapour trails.

CLOUD TYPES

Clouds can look totally different from one day to the next, as the weather changes. We usually describe clouds by their height in the sky and their shape.

HIGHEST CLOUDS

The highest clouds in the troposphere form between 5–13 kilometres above the ground. At this height, the atmosphere is very cold, so these clouds are the result of sublimation of water vapour into ice crystals. They are called cirrus clouds, from the Latin word for curl. They are usually shaped like wisps or curls of hair blown in the same direction by the wind.

CUMULUS CLOUDS

Clouds in the cumulus group look a little like flat-bottomed, heaped balls of cotton wool, or cauliflower. These are the clouds that often form over mountains or over warm land or ocean during summer. The flat bottoms mark the level at which the dew point is reached.

Sometimes, cumulus clouds form rows. When the rows are high in the sky they are called cirrocumulus clouds. Occasionally, cirrocumulus clouds bunch together giving a mackerel sky, so-called because the pattern is a little like the skin on a mackerel fish. Cumulus clouds found low down in the sky, at around 5 kilometres, are called altocumulus. When cumulus clouds are very low in the sky and form clumpy layers, they are called stratocumulus.

◀ Cirrus clouds usually form against blue skies on hot, clear days. These are clouds that generally do not signal wet weather.

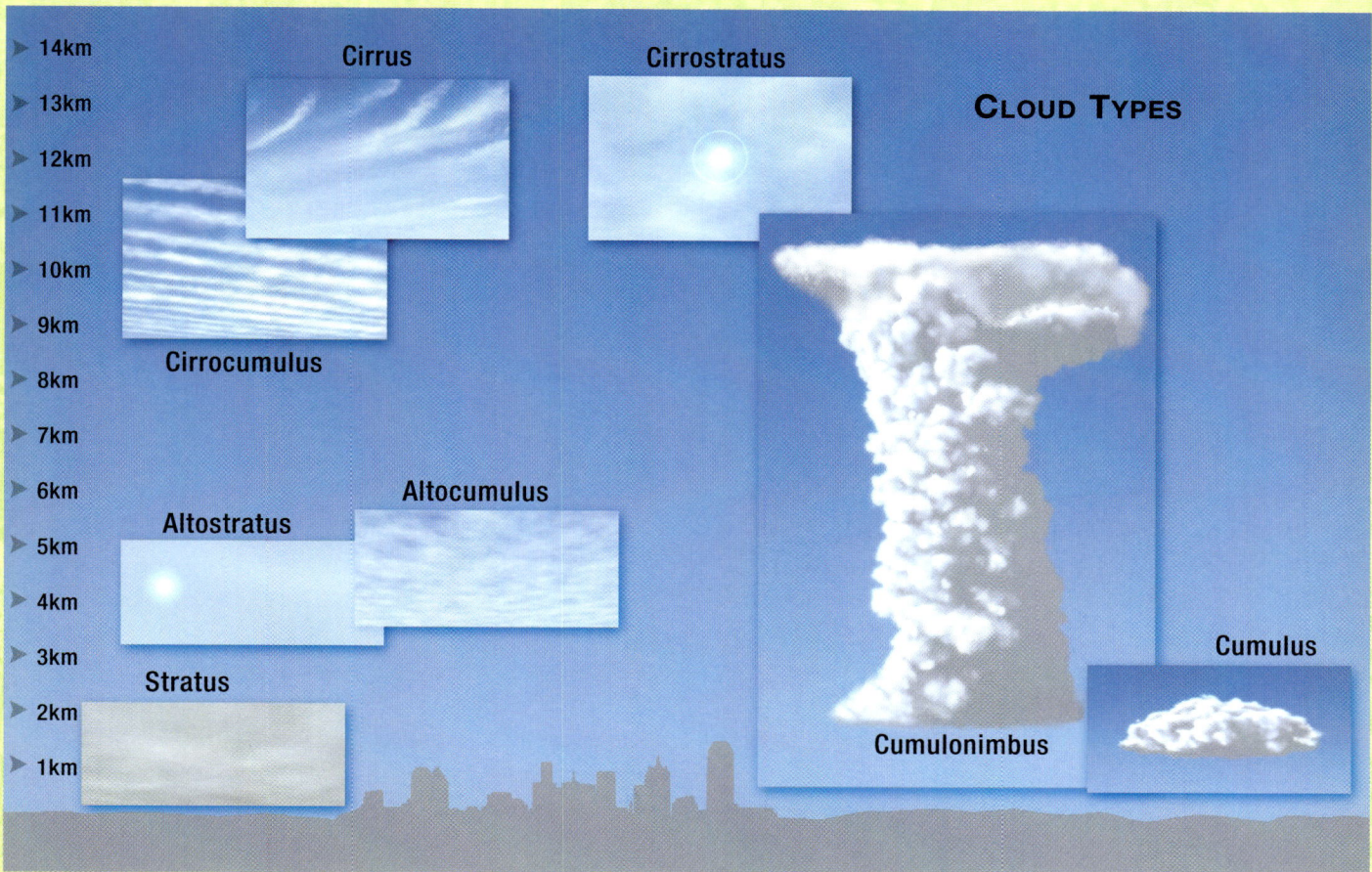

14km	Cirrus — Cirrostratus — **CLOUD TYPES**
13km	
12km	
11km	
10km	
9km	Cirrocumulus
8km	
7km	
6km	Altocumulus
5km	Altostratus
4km	
3km	Cumulus
2km	Stratus
1km	Cumulonimbus

▲ Some of the different types of cloud, and the heights they form above the ground.

The tallest cumulus clouds, cumulonimbus clouds, may extend 6–8 kilometres through the troposphere. They form when a cumulus cloud is added to by more and more rising warm air. As they heap up vertically, the air within them becomes saturated with water droplets lower down and ice crystals higher up. Nimbus is the Latin word for rain, and these clouds usually bring wet weather.

BLANKET CLOUDS

Stratus clouds are named after the Latin word for layer. They appear as featureless, grey blankets of cloud, usually less than 1.6 kilometres above the ground. Stratus clouds are grey, because they are saturated with rain droplets that let little sunlight through. These clouds form when cumulus clouds close together. They often appear over high ground. Mountaineers and hikers may struggle to see where they are in a thick stratus cloud. Stratus clouds typically bring damp, drizzly weather. However, the darkest grey stratus clouds – nimbostratus – always bring heavy rain.

HISTORY FOCUS

LUKE HOWARD (1772–1864)
Luke Howard was a British chemist by profession, but also an amateur weather enthusiast. He became interested in clouds after seeing the amazing skies that followed volcanic eruptions in Iceland in 1783. At that time, people described clouds as looking like other things, for example, mare's tails or castles. In 1802, Howard published a classification of cloud types he had observed. His simple, accurate descriptions were widely used, and are still the basis of cloud identification today.

PRECIPITATION

Precipitation is water that falls from the atmosphere as drizzle, rain, snow, hail or sleet. The different kinds of precipitation are part of the water cycle.

SHORT, SHARP SHOWERS

Short bursts of precipitation happen after small droplets of water in a cloud bump into each other and merge into bigger ones. This process is called coalescence. Droplets coalesce as air currents blow them upwards. At the top of a cloud, the enlarged droplets become heavy enough to fall. The largest of these raindrops fall fast from the cloud. The smallest raindrops, although around 100 times bigger than a water droplet, are very light. Most of these evaporate as they fall slowly through the warmer air below the cloud.

Sometimes, fast, upward winds inside clouds blow raindrops so high that they freeze. Frozen raindrops are called hailstones. A hailstone gets bigger when more water droplets freeze onto the outside of it.

◀ Short, heavy bursts of rain usually fall from tall clouds in which there is lots of height for droplets to rise and coalesce (come together).

FACT FOCUS

LAYERS OF ICE

Hailstones form when frozen rain from high in a cloud falls down inside enormous cumulonimbus clouds. When hailstones meet water droplets at the warmer bottom of the cloud, the water freezes slowly into a clear layer of ice on the cold hail. Rising air can carry the hail back up and the process is repeated, thereby making it bigger. At the colder top of the cloud the adding of new layers happens more quickly, forming a layer of white ice. Scientists count the number of layers in hailstones to see how often they have travelled up and down the cloud.

▲ Larger, wetter snowflakes with complicated shapes like this form when the air is near freezing. Simpler, powdery snowflakes form when it is even colder.

LONG, STEADY PRECIPITATION

Long, steady rain, snow and drizzle start life as ice crystals in cold clouds. The crystals move around slowly and bump into very cold water droplets. The water vapour condenses and slowly freezes onto the crystals. In this way, snowflakes gradually grow bigger. Eventually, they grow heavy enough to fall out of the cloud. If they travel through cold air, they remain frozen and fall as snowflakes. If they fall through warm air, they melt and form raindrops. This usually happens from low clouds, such as nimbostratus. When raindrops are as small as a full stop on this page, they are called drizzle.

WATER CYCLE

Nearly all of the water that falls to Earth ends up in the atmosphere again and again. Most precipitation runs off the surface of the land into streams and rivers, even if it remains frozen for a while first. Most water that soaks into the soil to become groundwater (water stored in soil or gaps in rock under the ground) eventually seeps into rivers. All of this surface and groundwater flows into the oceans. Some water evaporates from the surface of oceans, lakes, rivers and reservoirs, and this water vapour eventually forms clouds and precipitation, which falls back to Earth completing the cycle. This movement of water between land, ocean and atmosphere is called the water cycle.

Snow Clouds Rain Condensation Surface water Lake THE WATER CYCLE Evaporation Groundwater Sea

▲ The water cycle is powered by heat energy that evaporates water. The heat comes from infrared radiation in the Sun's rays.

THUNDER AND LIGHTNING

Thunderstorms come from giant cumulonimbus clouds and bring heavy rain. The noisy thunderclaps we hear, and the lightning flashes that light up the skies, are caused by a build-up of electrical charges in the cloud.

ELECTRICAL CHARGES

Cumulonimbus clouds usually form during spells of hot weather. Warm, humid air rises very fast and cools rapidly. Turbulence in these clouds causes ice crystals and raindrops to swirl around and crash into each other. This creates friction (a force that slows down movement and creates heat when two objects rub against each other), which charges the

▼ Lightning takes the shortest route from clouds to ground – such as through tall buildings and trees.

particles with static electricity. The smaller crystals tend to develop positive charges and are light enough to be blown to the top of the cumulonimbus. Raindrops and hailstones develop negative charges. They are heavier and fall to the bottom of the cloud.

THUNDER AND LIGHTNING

Positive and negative charges attract each other. When enormous electrical charges build up in cumulonimbus clouds we see the force of this attraction as movement of a giant electrical spark – a flash of lightning. Sheet lightning happens when the spark leaps between different parts of the cloud, lighting up the inside of it. Forked lightning happens between the bottom of the cloud and the ground. The negative charge in the cloud base causes the ground beneath it to have a positive charge, and a spark passes between them.

Lightning is so intensely hot that it heats the air in front of it up to 30,000°C as it travels. Thunder is the noise made when the air around the lightning suddenly expands in the heat. The reason we hear a thunderclap after we see a flash of lightning is that sound travels more slowly than light.

▲ Thunderclouds can release such a vast quantity of rain over a short period of time that they often cause flooding.

EVIDENCE FOCUS

MAKING LIGHTNING

You can make an electrical spark, such as a mini flash of lightning, at home. Stick a big lump of modelling clay to the middle of a large baking tray, and stand the tray on a big plastic bag. Holding the clay, rub the tray round and round on the bag, ideally in a dark room. Then, pick up the tray (using the clay as a handle) and hold a metal object, such as a tin lid, close to one corner of the tray. You should see a spark of static electricity jump from the tray to the metal.

THUNDERCLOUDS

Cumulonimbus clouds can reach the height of the tallest mountains. They look very grey, dark and heavy, because the air inside is so saturated with water that very little sunlight can get through. Thunderclouds may contain up to 5,000 million litres of water, which is enough to fill 130 Olympic-size swimming pools. Raindrops or hailstones that fall from the tall cumulonimbus clouds can be very large. Each raindrop falls, coalescing with other droplets of water on the way down, and then may be relifted by upward moving air to fall again. This can happen several times and the raindrop grows larger each time.

WIND

Wind is air that moves over the Earth's surface from areas of high pressure to areas of low pressure. Two things cause differences in air pressure: changes in temperature and the rotation of the Earth.

HOW WINDS FORM

Changes in air temperature cause differences in air pressure and create wind. Cool air creates areas of high pressure, because it is denser than warm air and sinks, pushing down on Earth, causing air below to be pushed out of the way. Warm air rises, creating an area of low pressure. Gases always try to move from

▼ There is always an area of high pressure above the icy Antarctic region. Winds blow fast here as air near the surface is squashed out by cold air sinking down from above.

areas of high pressure to areas of low pressure. You can remember this by the phrase: 'Winds blow from high to low'. The greater the difference between high and low pressure areas in a part of the atmosphere, the greater the wind speeds.

EARTH'S ROTATION AND WIND

One of the reasons air pressure varies from place to place is the rotation of the Earth. As the Earth spins on its axis, it drags air in the lower part of the atmosphere with it. The air higher in the atmosphere is less affected by the

Earth's rotation. This means that the air at different levels of the atmosphere is moving at different speeds. This causes turbulence in the atmosphere, which you sometimes feel when you are flying in an airplane, and helps to create winds at ground level.

WINDS AROUND THE WORLD

Local wind patterns occur because of pressure differences in the immediate area, but there are global wind patterns, too. Warm air rising high into the air above the hot regions north and south of the Equator forms winds that blow towards the poles. Lower, cold winds blow from the poles towards the low-pressure Equator.

As the Earth rotates, the Equator spins faster than the poles. This deflects the basic north-to-south and south-to-north flow of air. It causes characteristic patterns of wind direction in the northern and southern hemispheres. Winds that blow from around 30 degrees latitude towards the Equator are known as the trade winds. They blow from the north-east in the northern hemisphere and from the south-east in

▲ Wind turbines harness the wind's movement energy and convert it into electrical energy.

the southern hemisphere. Winds that blow from 30–60 degrees latitude towards the poles are called westerlies. They blow from the south-west in the northern hemisphere and from the north-west in the southern hemisphere.

EVIDENCE FOCUS

UNDER PRESSURE

When you inflate a balloon, you force a lot of air inside it. This air is compressed, or squashed together, so it is at high pressure. If you let go of the end of the balloon, the air inside rushes out and the balloon flies around the room. The air has moved from inside, where it was under high pressure, to outside where the pressure is lower.

WINDS AROUND THE WORLD

As well as the trade winds, there are other predictable winds that affect the weather. Jet streams blow high in the atmosphere, reaching speeds of over 326 kilometres an hour. And the monsoon creates wet and dry seasons in parts of Asia.

▲ When monsoon rains flood fields, farmers can sow rice plants, which can only grow in water.

MONSOON WINDS

In April and May, it is very hot in India, and other parts of Asia, and an area of low pressure develops over the land. The ocean takes longer to warm up than the land, so above the ocean there is an area of high pressure. The monsoon winds blow from the high-pressure area towards the low-pressure area inland. These winds are full of water vapour that has evaporated into the air over the warm Indian Ocean. The vapour rises, cools and condenses, especially over mountainous areas such as the Himalayas. Torrential rain falls in a short monsoon season. In winter, the land loses heat more quickly than the ocean, so the situation reverses. The wind blows out to sea, leaving dry sunny weather in Asia.

JET STREAMS

Jet streams are fast flowing paths of air that blow in the upper atmosphere. They are formed by temperature differences in the troposphere, between layers of cold air from above the poles and layers of warm air from above the Equator. This big change in temperature causes a large pressure difference,

JET STREAMS

'Jet streams' were first discovered during the Second World War, when pilots flying planes between the UK and the USA noticed it was quicker to fly to the UK. This was because they could get blown along on the 'rivers' of fast-flowing air moving from west to east, which became known as jet streams.

which forces the air to move. Jet stream winds form long tubes of air that run between the bands of warm and cold air. The movement of air in the jet streams starts to form areas

▼ The Mistral wind is strong enough to cause direct damage. It can also cause indirect damage, as here, by fanning small fires into giant blazes.

of high pressure and low pressure in the atmosphere, and these create changes in our weather.

LOCAL WINDS

Local winds can have significant effects on weather in different parts of the world. For example, during the winter in France, high-pressure air builds up above the Alps. This becomes the Mistral wind as it flows downhill fast towards a low-pressure area over the warm Mediterranean Sea. The Mistral's name comes from a French word for 'master': this cold, harsh wind roars through the Rhône Valley, often causing serious damage.

The Chinook wind in the USA develops when air is forced upwards over the Rocky Mountains and loses its moisture. When it suddenly drops down again, on the other side of the Rockies, it is compressed and becomes warm. The resulting hot, dry wind can melt snow very quickly – chinook means 'snow-eater' in a local Native American language.

AIR MASSES

Air masses are huge volumes of air with the same temperature and humidity. Different air masses appear over the coldest and hottest areas of Earth. They move around the planet, changing the weather as they go.

HOW AIR MASSES FORM

A band of air warms up or cools down when it rests above the Earth's surface. Tropical air masses are warm air masses that form after resting above or near the Equator. Polar air masses form over the Arctic and Antarctic ice. Air masses become more humid when they rest on oceans than they do on land. Water from ocean surfaces evaporates, forming water vapour. More than two-thirds of our planet is covered in ocean, so the largest air masses are humid ones.

▼ The summer weather in Australia is hot and dry because a dry tropical air mass rests over the centre of this continent.

▲ The severe rains caused by El Niño turned soil to mud on mountain slopes above this Californian town. The mud slid and buried whole streets.

Air masses move around the world, carried by winds. Tropical air masses generally move away from the Equator and polar air masses move towards the Equator. As air masses move, they warm up, cool down, get drier, or more humid, according to the part of the Earth's surface they move over and the time of year.

POLAR FRONTS

Fronts are imaginary lines where different air masses meet. Polar fronts are where tropical and polar air masses meet. For example, in the USA, the polar front lies along a line roughly between California and New England. In winter, a cold, dry polar air mass moves from the Arctic down through North America bringing cold, dry weather. A humid tropical air mass brings warm, wet weather off the Caribbean Sea. At the polar front there is unsettled weather because the air masses generally do not mix together. Instead, they form pockets of warm or cold air that bring variable weather.

UNUSUAL WEATHER

The movement of air masses usually creates typical weather patterns in different parts of the world. However, sometimes air masses move differently, causing unusual weather. For example, a humid tropical air mass normally forms above warm Pacific Ocean water near Australia and Indonesia. It causes wet weather. The warm water is held there by westerly trade winds. However, every two to seven years, around Christmas, the winds drop or even change direction. The warm water and humid air then move eastwards to the other side of the Pacific Ocean. This change is called El Niño. It transforms weather around the Pacific.

WEATHER SYSTEMS

Air masses with different air pressures create weather systems where they meet. These are typical patterns of cloud, rain and wind that change as fronts move.

CYCLONES

Cyclones are areas of low air pressure around which air slowly rotates. They happen when warm air rises. Winds spiral around the centre of a cyclone and into it. Their speed depends on the pressure difference between the centre of the cyclone and the edges. Cyclones are called depressions in some parts of the world. The weather in most cyclones is cloudy and wet, because the warm rising air cools and its moisture condenses.

ANTICYCLONES

Anticyclones are areas of high air pressure. They generally affect larger areas and last longer than cyclones. Air slowly sinks into the centre of an anticyclone, causing mild winds to blow spirally outwards. This movement of air can block the movement of cyclones into an area.

▶ In winter, anticyclones can bring very low night-time temperatures because there are few clouds to trap air warmed during the day close to the Earth.

▲ The cold air sinking into an anticyclone compresses the air. No clouds can form because the air is dried out and warmed up, especially in summer.

Anticyclones usually bring long periods of dry, clear weather over a wide area. Sinking air can meet cooler air underneath and create a temperature inversion. Then, frost or fog may form as water vapour freezes or condenses.

WEATHER FRONTS

While a front is a general boundary between air masses, there are points along its length where warm air bulges over the cold air. This causes the pressure to drop at the Earth's surface. The area of lowest pressure is a depression. Higher pressure cold air from an anticyclone spirals into the depression. It squeezes the warm air sharply up.

The line where the warm air pushes against the cold air is a warm front. When a warm front approaches, cirrus clouds appear, followed by cumulus, and finally stratus clouds bringing some rain. It can get windy. The temperature rises when the warm front passes over and the air is stiller.

The line where the cold air pushes against the warm air is called a cold front. When a cold front arrives, the temperature drops and there are strong gusts of winds. Heavy showers of rain or snow fall from cumulonimbus clouds. These clouds are caused by rapid cooling of warm air that is being forced up into the atmosphere from underneath. Once the cold front passes, the sky clears.

▼ You can spot an advancing cold front by a line of towering rain clouds and even rain falling. In the northern hemisphere, cold fronts generally move eastwards.

TROPICAL STORMS AND TORNADOES

Tropical storms and tornadoes are the most destructive weather systems on Earth. They are extreme cyclones that happen when very warm, humid air spins fast and rises powerfully into the atmosphere.

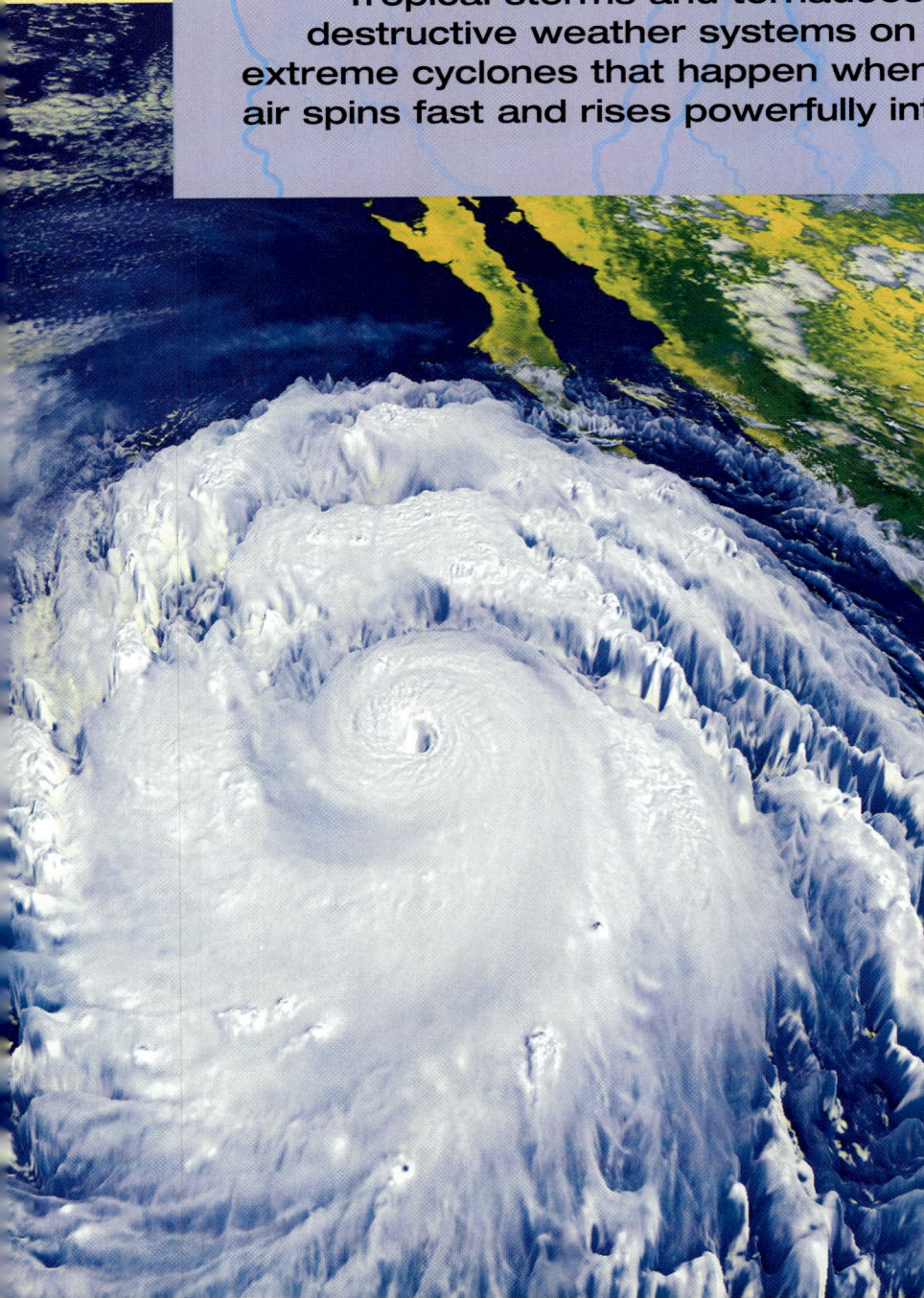

TROPICAL STORMS

Tropical storms form over warm tropical seas during the hottest times of year. When air is warmer than 26°C and saturated with water vapour it rises fast into the atmosphere. Humid trade winds rush into the low-pressure gap left beneath, and also rise. Strong winds start to blow upwards around the cyclone centre. Cumulus and cumulonimbus clouds form quickly as the humid air cools. The winds and clouds spin around the storm centre owing to the Coriolis force, the force that results from the rotation of the Earth around its axis.

The centre of a tropical storm is called the eye and usually measures 30–60 kilometres across. In the eye, the air is calm, cloudless, and about 3°C warmer than other parts of the storm. Around the eye, there is a wall of cloud rotating at wind speeds of up to 350 kilometres per hour. That's as fast as the quickest train.

▲ This satellite photo clearly shows the anticlockwise spiralling clouds and clear eye of a hurricane moving over an ocean.

TROPICAL STORMS

Tropical storms are unstoppable. When people are warned that one is coming their way, they may even evacuate their homes to avoid danger. Scientists are working on ways to stop them forming in the first place. One method is to get airplanes to drop silver iodide crystals into growing storm clouds. Water vapour condenses rapidly and coalesces on the crystals, causing rain, instead of enlarging the cloud. This is called seeding clouds.

TROPICAL STORMS AROUND THE WORLD

Tropical storms are usually called hurricanes over the north Atlantic and north-east Pacific Oceans. Hurricanes usually move north and west across the Caribbean Sea and the Gulf of Mexico. Hurricanes always spin anticlockwise but, in the southern hemisphere, tropical storms spin clockwise. Tropical storms that form over the west Pacific and Indian Oceans are usually called typhoons, willy-willies or cyclones.

Tropical storms travel at around 10 kilometres per hour. They get their energy from warm, humid air over the ocean, so they fizzle out when they move over drier land.

TORNADOES

Tornadoes, or whirlwinds, are smaller, faster and shorter-lived than tropical storms. They form over flat land during storms when warm, humid winds spiral above cold, dry winds. The warm air spins as fast as a jet plane up into cumulonimbus clouds. The cold air condenses the water vapour, so the rising warm air appears as a funnel of cloud reaching down to the Earth's surface. The very low pressure in the eye of a tornado sucks up not only more humid air, but also anything else, from dust from the ground and water from lakes, to trees, houses and cars.

▼ Tornadoes are often called twisters because the funnel zigzags over land. They can travel hundreds of kilometres before they run out of warm air.

WEATHER STATIONS

There are weather stations all over the world. Meteorologists (scientists who study the weather) use different instruments to collect weather data 24 hours a day, 7 days a week, from land, sea and in the air.

ON THE GROUND

Weather stations on the ground use a variety of instruments to observe the weather. Rain gauges measure precipitation in millimetres. Thermometers record daily maximum and minimum temperatures, as well as current temperatures, and barometers measure air pressure. In many places, a simple wind sock tells the direction of the wind, and an instrument called an anemometer measures how fast the wind is blowing. Humidity is measured using a special kind of thermometer known as a hygrometer. Sunlight is focused onto sensitive paper to trace how many hours of sunshine there were in a day, and cloud cover is recorded by observation alone.

▼ This meteorologist is collecting weather data from instruments on a tower high above the Amazonian rainforest.

WEATHER SAYINGS

Long before weather forecasts, people made up sayings based on their observations to help them predict the weather. Many are true. Here are two examples.

- 'Rain before seven quits before eleven'; fronts that bring rain usually last about six hours, although they can happen any time, not just in the mornings.

- 'The bigger the ring, the nearer the rain'; sometimes, sunlight is bent through the ice crystals in cirrus clouds, forming a halo of light around the Sun or Moon. The halo gets wider when more crystals in thicker, moisture-filled clouds bend more light. As the clouds grow, rain is more likely.

▲ When a weather balloon reaches 20 kilometres in the sky it bursts and a parachute opens to float the instruments back to Earth.

AT SEA

Much of our information about weather at sea is collected by offshore weather buoys, which are either moored off a coast or drift out at sea. These have sensors and instruments that collect atmospheric information including air pressure, air temperature and wind direction and speed. Many of these are similar to those used on land. They also record data about the ocean water, such as temperature, wave heights and currents. Similar kinds of information are also gathered from ships at sea. Off the coasts of the USA there are the Coastal-Marine Automated Network (C-man) weather stations, built on lighthouses, islands, and on offshore oil-rig platforms.

IN THE AIR

One way of taking measurements in the atmosphere is with helium-filled weather balloons, also known as radiosondes. These carry instruments for measuring air temperature and humidity, and send back measurements by radio. After a radiosonde is launched, radars track it so meteorologists can measure wind speed and direction as it climbs through the atmosphere. Airplanes also gather weather information and are sometimes sent out to observe storms as they happen.

Weather satellites and weather radars measure weather conditions far away. Radars send out energy beams that hit rain, snow and sleet. They tell how far away the weather is by measuring the time taken for the beam to bounce back. Radars are useful for tracking storms. Pictures taken by satellites in space show clouds, snow cover and movements of weather systems such as hurricanes. Satellites can also take infrared images that are colour-enhanced to show temperatures on the ground.

WEATHER FORECASTS

Data from weather stations feed into powerful computers. Meteorologists use these computers to analyse the data and to produce weather charts and maps predicting weather to come.

▲ Weather forecasters use banks of different computers to analyse and visualise changes in weather data over time.

SYNOPTIC CHARTS

Information collected by weather stations around a country is sent to a central computer. Meteorologists then use this information to compile a special weather map called a synoptic chart. The location of each weather station is marked on this map, alongside coded numbers and symbols that indicate the weather information they sent. Meteorologists then draw in the isobars and fronts to create a picture of the current weather systems across a country.

FACT FOCUS

A VARIETY OF FORECASTS
Weather forecasters produce different reports for different people. There are surfers' reports that give wave height and wind speed and directions at popular coastal surfing spots. And, in some countries, meteorological offices provide local forecasts where golfers can find out what the weather will be like on a particular course by pressing a button on their mobile phone.

Isobars are lines on a synoptic chart that join areas that have the same air pressure. You will see isobars on maps of weather forecasts in newspapers, too. The closer together isobars are, the more rapidly the air pressure changes from place to place and, therefore, the stronger the winds.

PREDICTING THE WEATHER

Meteorologists then use the information they have from synoptic charts, satellite pictures and their knowledge of weather patterns in the past to predict what will happen next. They use computers to analyse all the factors influencing the weather in a place to work out what weather that place will have over the coming days. For example, if wind direction is such that a cold front is blowing towards an area, that means heavy rain is on the way. They also produce long-range forecasts that can predict general weather patterns months in advance.

WEATHER SIGNS AND SYMBOLS

Weather forecasters need to present weather information in a way everyone can understand. Some television forecasts use animated 3-D images of rain or clouds moving across an aerial view of a country. Many weather forecasts use picture symbols to show weather features such as sunshine, clouds, rain and thunder. They show wind speed and temperatures as numbers in circles. Areas of high and low pressure are marked high or low. Fronts are shown as curved lines that bend in the direction that the wind is moving.

▼ These are some of the symbols you need to know to understand a weather map.

WEATHER FORECAST SYMBOLS

Sunny	Sunny intervals	Drizzle or light rain

Heavy rain	Thundery shower	Tropical storm

Cold front	Warm front	Isobars
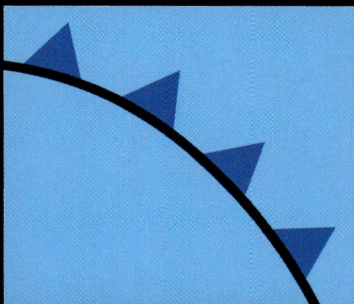	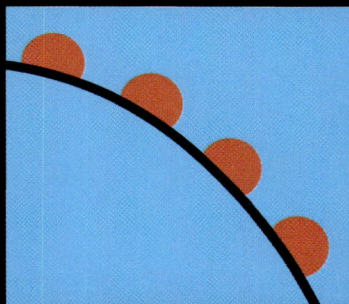	

GLOBAL WEATHER PROBLEMS

Some human activities have created changes to the Earth's atmosphere that affect aspects of our weather. Examples include the destruction of the ozone layer and the formation of acid rain and serious smog.

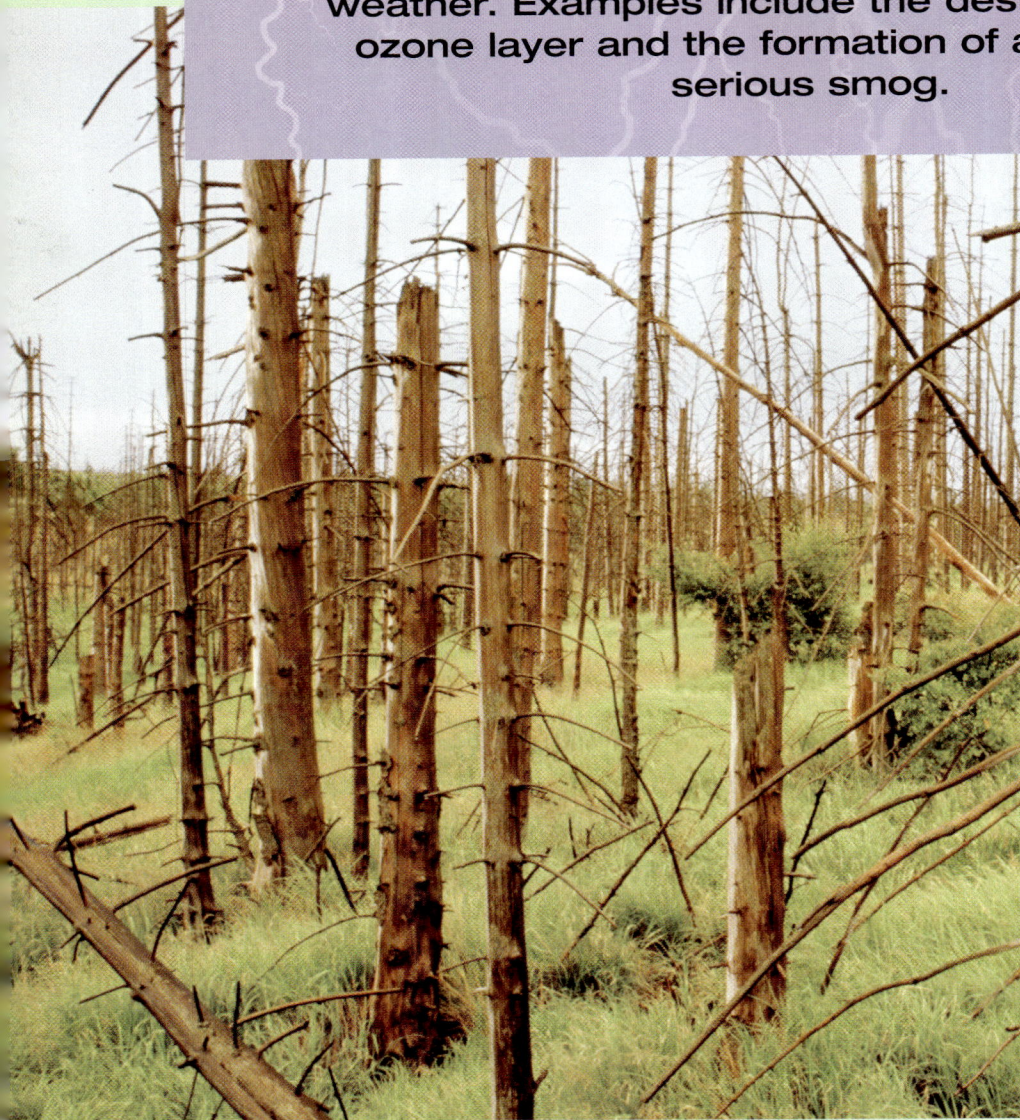

ACID RAIN

Rainwater is usually slightly acidic, because it mixes with carbon dioxide in the atmosphere. However, it becomes even more acidic when people alter the balance of gases in the atmosphere. The burning of fossil fuels such as oil, coal or gas in power stations, factories and vehicles releases large amounts of carbon dioxide, sulphur dioxide and nitrogen oxide gas into the atmosphere. When these gases dissolve in raindrops as they fall through the air, they make the rain as strongly acidic as lemon juice. Acid rain kills trees when it falls on forests. It may poison fish and other aquatic animals when it flows into rivers and lakes, or it may dissolve the limestone of some buildings.

▲ Acid rain affects trees in two ways. It damages their leaves so they cannot make food by photosynthesis. It also accumulates in the soil, making it more difficult for roots to take in the nutrients trees need to grow.

OZONE HOLES

In 1985, scientists discovered a hole in the ozone layer over Antarctica, and during the 1990s another hole appeared over the North Pole. These holes are not really holes, but regions where there is a lower than normal concentration of ozone gas.

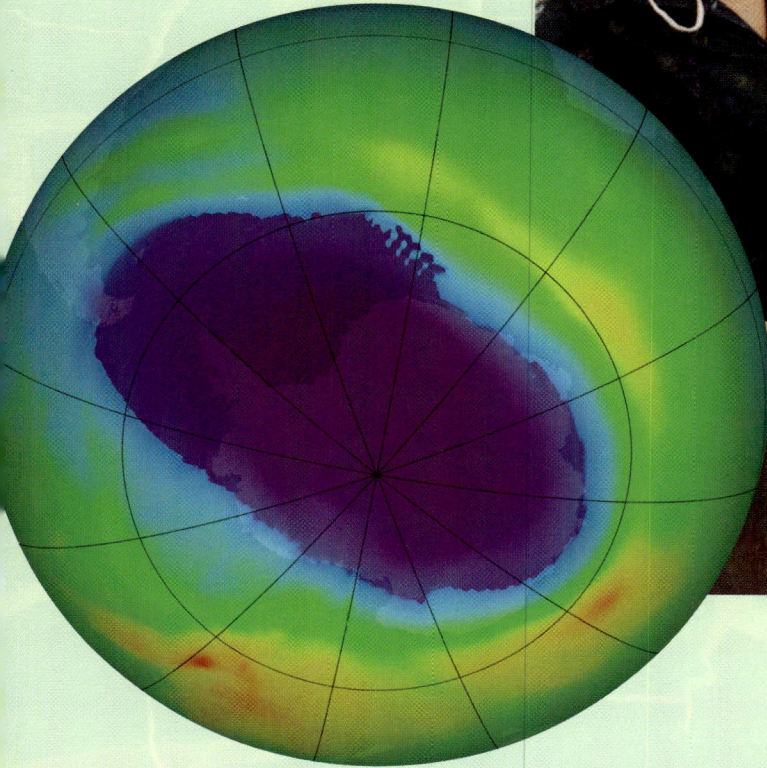

▼ This image of the Antarctica ozone hole (in dark blue) was made using data collected by a satellite that can detect ozone amounts in the atmosphere.

▲ In 1997, forest fires caused terrible smog to linger over Indonesia for months. Schools and airports were forced to close and tens of thousands of people suffered serious breathing problems.

Scientists believe that gases used in refrigerators, aerosol cans and foam packaging have damaged the atmosphere and created these holes. They hope that a world ban on the use of these chemicals since 1987 may help the ozone layer to heal. In the meantime, the damage has dangerously reduced the amount of protection the ozone layer gives us from harmful ultraviolet radiation.

SMOG

Smog is polluted air that forms a brown or yellowish haze, usually over cities in summertime. Smog is often held close to the Earth's surface by temperature inversion. One of the main polluting gases in smog is ozone. Ozone is useful in the atmosphere, but at ground level it can be harmful to us. Polluting gases from factories, vehicles and oil-based products, such as paint, create ozone. These chemical gases react together with sunlight and heat to create ozone gas. The ozone in smog can cause breathing problems in people and damage trees and other plants.

FACT FOCUS

WEATHERING

Weathering is when sun, wind and rain gradually wear away stone. Over many thousands of years weathering can create caves and arches in limestone rock. Acid rain greatly speeds up limestone weathering and, sadly, some historic buildings and sculptures made from limestone are disappearing because of it.

CLIMATE CHANGE

Throughout the Earth's history climate has naturally changed, growing gradually hotter or colder for long periods of time. Today, many scientists believe that the climate is warming up much faster than ever before.

CLIMATE CHANGE IN THE PAST

Around 450 million years ago the hot, dry area that is now the Sahara Desert was covered in ice, because the African continent was then positioned over today's South Pole. Over the last two million years, most places on Earth have experienced ice ages every 100,000 years or so.

▼ Industrial air pollution has only been around since the late eighteenth century, when people started to harness the energy from fossil fuels.

The climate has cooled for thousands of years, and then warmed up again.

Scientists know climates were different in the distant past from evidence in rocks and fossils. For example, if a plant fossil from a desert is similar to plants that thrive in cold places today, then the area was probably once much colder. Some landforms, such as U-shaped valleys carved by glaciers, could only have formed when the climate was cold.

GLOBAL CLIMATE CHANGE

Since 1860, the average temperature on Earth has risen by 0.6°C. This does not sound like much, but for many people it is evidence of global warming. The Earth keeps warm because of the greenhouse effect of gases such as carbon dioxide and methane in its atmosphere. Today, the atmosphere is trapping more warmth than in the previous 10,000 years because there are more of these gases in it than ever before.

People release carbon dioxide when they burn fossil fuels. The amount of carbon dioxide we release is exceeding the amount plants can use up in photosynthesis, so it stays in the atmosphere. The increasing numbers of farm livestock in the world release lots of methane. The extra gases mean less heat can escape from near the Earth's surface.

EFFECTS OF CLIMATE CHANGE

The effects of climate change are many. An increase in temperatures on land means more heatwaves, droughts and forest fires. An increase in ocean temperatures means more hurricanes and greater levels of evaporation, which creates fuller clouds that blow inland, bringing heavy rain and floods. Global climate change is also melting ice sheets at the poles, which causes a rise in sea levels around the world. This causes floods at some coastal areas and may permanently cover low-lying islands and coastal countries in future.

▶ Scientists predict that sea levels will rise by between 9 and 88cm by 2100. That would be enough to submerge the low-lying Maldive Islands in the Indian Ocean.

TIMELINE

Here are some of the main discoveries and milestones in the history of weather.

1492 Genoese seaman, explorer and adventurer Christopher Columbus discovers the trade winds while sailing across the Atlantic Ocean.

1593 Galileo Galilei invents a water thermometer that can measure temperature variations.

1686 English astronomer Edmund Halley publishes his study of trade winds and monsoons. He determines that the Sun's energy warming air creates atmospheric motion.

1724 Gabriel Fahrenheit creates a reliable scale for measuring temperature with a mercury-type thermometer (°F).

1742 Swedish astronomer Anders Celsius proposes the centigrade temperature scale, which leads to the current Celsius scale (°C).

1806 British admiral Francis Beaufort develops his scale of wind speed.

1835 Gaspard-Gustave Coriolis recognises that the rotation of Earth causes a small velocity-dependent force, now called the Coriolis force.

1843 Samuel Morse invents the first long-distance electric telegraph line, allowing weather information to be exchanged more quickly than ever before.

1860 Five hundred US telegraph stations are making weather observations and submitting them back to the Smithsonian Institution. The observations are later interrupted by the Civil War.

1861 Francis Galton produces the first modern weather map.

1870 Level of carbon dioxide in the atmosphere reaches 290 ppm (parts per million).

1886 Swedish chemist Svante Arrhennius publishes first scientific paper on global warming caused by human air pollution.

1891 Norway tracks first signs of acid rain on its western coast.

1898 President William McKinley orders the US Weather Bureau to establish a hurricane warning network in the West Indies.

1912 As a result of the sinking of the ship *Titanic* by an iceberg, an international ice patrol is established, conducted by the Coast Guard service.

1913 The ozone layer is discovered by Charles Fabry.

1918 German botanist and climatologist Vladimir Koppen develops a classification system for world climate regions.

1922 Hottest ever recorded temperature on Earth of 58°C in Libya.

1934–37 The Dust Bowl drought of the US plains region causes harsh economic damage.

1937 The term 'greenhouse effect' is first coined by American assistant professor Glen Thomas Trewartha.

1945 Second World War pilots discover jet streams.

1950 The World Meteorological Organisation (WMO) is established by the United Nations to coordinate weather data and information collected from countries around the world.

1952 The wettest single day ever recorded when 1,870 litres per square metre of rain fall on the Pacific island of La Réunion.

1957 Oceanographer Roger Revelle finds that carbon dioxide produced by humans will not be readily absorbed by the oceans.

1960 Level of carbon dioxide in the atmosphere reaches 315 ppm.

1960 First weather satellite, Tiros 1, is launched into space.

1969 Saffir-Simpson Hurricane Scale is created, used to describe hurricane strength on a category range of 1 to 5.

1970 Largest hailstone ever recorded on Earth falls in Kansas, USA. It weighs 768g and is the size of a small melon.

1983 Lowest temperature ever recorded on Earth is −89.2°C in Antarctica.

1985 Discovery of hole in the ozone layer over Antarctica.

1986 Hailstones weighing 1kg fall in Gopalgani, Bangladesh.

1988 Second hole in the ozone layer is discovered over the Arctic.

1988 Level of carbon dioxide in the atmosphere reaches 350 ppm.

1990 A UN report on climate change warns that global temperatures might rise by more than 1.1°C in 35 years. The report recommends reducing carbon dioxide emissions worldwide.

1992 Earth Summit in Rio de Janeiro, Brazil, at which industrialised countries aim to reduce greenhouse gas emissions by 2000.

1997 The Kyoto Protocol makes it a legal requirement for industrialised nations to cut greenhouse gas emissions by 5 per cent by 2010. The treaty could only come into effect when countries accounting for 55 per cent of world greenhouse gas emissions signed up to it. The USA refused to sign, but when Russia signed it in 2005 the treaty came into force.

1998 The hottest year ever recorded.

2005 Level of carbon dioxide in the atmosphere reaches 380 ppm.

2020 Mount Kilimanjaro in Africa predicted to have no snow on top any more as a result of global warming.

2100 The Maldive Islands in the Indian Ocean could have disappeared owing to sea-level rise from global warming.

GLOSSARY

Acid rain Rainwater that has been polluted by chemicals in the air, especially industrial waste gases.

Anticyclone Area of high pressure (sinking) air in the atmosphere.

Aspect Particular direction an object or place is facing.

Atom Smallest particle of a chemical element that can take part in chemical reactions.

Axis Earth's axis is an imaginary line that goes through the middle of the planet, from North Pole to South Pole.

Buoy Man-made object that floats at sea, usually moored in one spot as a marker.

Cancer Serious disease in which some of the cells in the body multiply very quickly, sometimes forming a lump called a tumour.

Coalesce To grow or fuse together.

Condensation When water turns from a gas (water vapour) to liquid water.

Coriolis force Force created by the rotation of the Earth that makes air currents bend to the right in the northern hemisphere and to the left in the southern hemisphere.

Cyclone Area of low pressure (rising) air in the atmosphere. Also called a depression.

Dew point Temperature at which water vapour condenses.

Drought Long period of time without rain or with too little rain.

Equator Imaginary line around the centre of the Earth.

Evaporation When a substance like water changes from a solid or a liquid into vapour (gas in air).

Fossil fuel Natural fuel such as oil, gas, or coal, which formed from the remains of ancient living things.

Friction Force that slows down movement and creates heat when two objects rub against each other.

Front Dividing line between a band of cold, low-pressure air and a band of warm, moist high-pressure air.

Global warming General rise in temperatures worldwide, caused by the greenhouse effect.

Gravity Invisible force that causes a large mass to attract a smaller one. A stick thrown into the air comes back to Earth because of gravity.

Greenhouse effect Gases in the atmosphere work like the glass in a greenhouse and trap warmth from the Sun, keeping Earth warm.

Groundwater Water stored in soil or gaps in rock under the ground.

High pressure Areas of cool air are heavier than warm air. They are said to create areas of high pressure because they press down more heavily towards the Earth.

Hurricane Severe and often destructive tropical cyclone bringing strong winds and heavy rains.

Infrared radiation Invisible rays in the air. The Sun's heat travels through space to Earth as infrared rays.

Latitude Distance north or south of the Earth's Equator.

Low pressure Areas of warm air are lighter than areas of cool air. They are said to create areas of low pressure because they press down less heavily towards the Earth.

Molecule The smallest amount of a chemical compound.

Nutrient A chemical that living things need to grow and survive.

Orbit The curved route of an object, such as a planet or satellite, around a larger object such as the Sun or a planet.

Ozone layer Layer of gas in the atmosphere that absorbs harmful radiation from sunlight hitting the Earth.

Photosynthesis Process by which plants make glucose in their leaves, using water, carbon dioxide from the air, and energy from sunlight.

Precipitation Water falling from the sky in liquid or solid form, such as rain or snow.

Prism Transparent object that can bend and separate light rays.

Radiation Movement of energy in the form of rays or waves we cannot see, such as heat and light from the Sun.

Satellite Object in space that sends out TV signals or takes photographs.

Static electricity When friction causes objects to be charged with electricity.

Sublimation When a substance changes between a frozen solid and a gas, without first becoming a liquid.

Temperature inversion When an upper layer of warm air in the troposphere traps cool air below at the surface.

Thermal Warm air current rising above a hot patch of ground.

Trade winds Cool winds that blow from the north and south towards the Equator.

Troposphere Layer of the atmosphere closest to Earth. It contains 90 per cent of the air in the atmosphere.

Turbulence Continuously changing air movement in the atmosphere, for example creating gusts of wind.

Ultraviolet (UV) radiation UV rays from the Sun. They are invisible but can cause sunburn.

Water cycle The continuous movement of water through the atmosphere, land, and ocean by processes of evaporation, condensation and precipitation.

Water vapour Water that has evaporated into the air and become a gas. Steam from a boiling kettle is a hot water vapour.

Weathering When rock is damaged or broken down by wind, rain or other kinds of weather.

FURTHER INFORMATION

Books to read

Awesome Forces of Nature: Howling Hurricanes and *Terrifying Tornadoes* by Richard and Louise Spilsbury (Heinemann Library, 2004)

Discovering Geography: Weather by Rebecca Hunter (Raintree, 2004)

Earth's Changing Landscapes: Weather and Climate by John Corn (Franklin Watts, 2004)

Earth Watch: Changing Climate by Sally Morgan (Franklin Watts, 2005)

Earth Watch: Ozone Hole by Sally Morgan (Franklin Watts, 2005)

Eyewitness: Weather by Brian Cosgrove (Dorling Kindersley, 2004)

Weather and Climate: Extreme Weather by Terry Jennings (Evans Brothers, 2005)

Websites

The Meteorological Office
www.metoffice.gov.uk/weather/index.html
Lots of information about weather around the world past and present, satellite views and climate prediction.

The US Geological Survey
http://ga.water.usgs.gov/edu/watercycle.html
A good explanation of the water cycle.

Clouds R Us.com
www.cloudsrus.com/
Not just about clouds – it covers all weather features with the help of activities. There is a useful FAQ section as well.

INDEX

Numbers shown in **bold** refer to pages with illustrations or photographs.